BULLS-EYE
NEGOTIATING

BY MARILYN JENNINGS

COPYRIGHT
1994 AND 1995 BY: MARILYN C. JENNINGS
P.O. BOX 6167, STN. "A"
CALGARY, AB, CANADA T2H 2L4
CANADA & USA   Dial 1-800-736-2335
NEW ZEALAND   Dial 0-800-449-702
AUSTRALIA   Dial 1-800-12-9096
E-MAIL: office@mcjpub.com
WEBSITE: www.mcjpub.com

PUBLISHED BY: MCJ PUBLISHING LTD.
P.O. BOX 6167, STN. "A"
CALGARY, AB, CANADA T2H 2L4
CANADA & USA   Dial 1-800-736-2335
NEW ZEALAND   Dial 0-800-449-702
AUSTRALIA   Dial 1-800-12-9096
E-MAIL: office@mcjpub.com
WEBSITE: www.mcjpub.com

PRINTED IN CANADA BY: EMERSON•CLARKE
PRINTING CORPORATION
9-4001B 19 STREET N.E.
CALGARY, ALBERTA
CANADA T2E 6X8

PRINTINGS: MCJ-07-94-2M-V1   MCJ-03-02-1.2M-V3
MCJ-03-95-1M-V1   MCJ-04-04-.7M-V3
MCJ-01-95-1M-V2   MCJ-07-05-.6M-V3
MCJ-01-96-1M-V2
MCJ-12-96-1M-V3
MCJ-11-97-.5M-V3
MCJ-07-00-1.1M-V3
MCJ-05-01-.6M-V3

Canadian Cataloguing in Publication Data

Jennings, Marilyn, 1943-

Bull's-Eye Negotiating

ISBN 0-9695115-1-5

1. Real estate business. 2. Negotiation in
business. I. Title.

HD1382.J46 J.994   333.33'068   C94-900493-6

ACKNOWLEDGMENTS

This book would not have been possible without the generous support of my husband Ed and my two daughters Sherri and Shelli.

I say a special "Thank You" to my long time associate Terry Reeder, who helped with the editing, sending manuscripts and letters all over the continent, co-ordinating the printing, artwork, packaging and all other aspects of the production process.

I'm deeply indebted to twenty-two of my colleagues in real estate sales across Canada and the United States, who read and critiqued the early manuscripts. These kind and busy souls approached this task with the enthusiasm you'd expect from someone negotiating their biggest sales commission ever, yet all they stood to gain from their efforts was a copy of this humble publication. Their constructive criticism and positive input was priceless. Without their generous assistance this project would have taken at least another year to complete.

I gratefully acknowledge the contribution of my friend and colleague, Sheila Francis from Coquitlam, British Columbia, Canada. In spite of being one of the top Real Estate Salespeople in North America and also one of the busiest, she generously took time out of her busy schedule to critique the manuscript a final time before it went to the typesetters.

I sincerely acknowledge the contributions of Tina Houston from Stewart Publishing, who was responsible for much of the editing and typesetting.

On more than one occasion Tina spent evenings and weekends producing revised versions of the manuscript so

I could review them before leaving on another extended speaking tour.

Last, but by no means least, I gratefully acknowledge the contributions of Mike Keller from Keller's Art Company who did the artwork on the dust cover; Paul Birnie from Appletree Photographic Arts for the photo on the dust cover and Peter Bolli, Brian Andersen and all the folks at Emerson Clarke Printing Corporation who had everything to do with the printing. These people have a way of making serious projects fun to complete and gave in excess of what they got paid to do to make this book a reality.

DEDICATION

DEDICATED TO MY
DARLING GRANDCHILDREN

JAYE, SPENCER, BRITTANY, BRAYDEN,
KEVIN AND JENESSA —
THE BEST LITTLE NEGOTIATORS
I'VE EVER KNOWN!

PREFACE

It's a fact that Real Estate Salespeople make their

living by negotiating with others. Although we often find ourselves negotiating with other parties involved in the same transactions as we are, primarily the negotiations we undertake are with, and on behalf of, Buyers and Sellers.

We start the negotiating process the minute we begin dealing with a prospect. We negotiate appointments for Buyer Interviews and Listing Presentations. We persuade people to sign Listing Agreements, Extension Agreements and Buyer Agency Agreements. We negotiate with people to make offers, accept offers, make counter-offers and accept counter-offers. We negotiate commissions, fees and retainers, bonuses, expiry dates and irrevocable dates on various types of agreements. The list goes on ad infinitum.

Those who enjoy a better batting average in all these aspects of real estate sales, are simply better negotiators than those with poorer averages. Obviously the better we become at negotiating these items — the more negotiating skills and techniques we can master — the more successful we'll be at the practice of our profession.

I've always been troubled by the fact that our industry does such a poor job of teaching salespeople how to become good negotiators. During my 30 years in the business, I've attended numerous industry sponsored courses, some of them mandatory, that were designed to make me a pseudo-lawyer; a pseudo-planner; a pseudo-construction expert; a pseudo-financial advisor; a pseudo-economist — anything but a better negotiator, salesperson and business person.

The last thing we teach licensees in this business, if we teach it to them at all, is how to make a living. To say this is a problem with our industry would be an understatement. The fact of the matter is, that it's a serious problem.

Whether we want to admit it or not, it's one of the main reasons why the turnover of salespeople in real estate sales is so outrageously high.

In most jurisdictions today the industry is prohibited by law, from fixing in any way the commission its members are allowed to charge for their services. That doesn't mean however, that we're prohibited from teaching salespeople and brokers how to become better negotiators, and that they have to charge enough for their services to earn a decent living and avoid bankruptcy. To think we can't do this without conspiring to fix commissions is absurdity in the extreme. Yet that seems to be the attitude adopted by the industry.

An interesting paradox emerges vis-a-vis the real estate industry, when we examine the evolution of negotiation as a field of academic interest. In one way, it's easy to understand why the industry has not done a better job of teaching salespeople to be good negotiators. On the other hand, one has to wonder why an industry having such a vital stake in the subject, hasn't played a leading role in the development of research, materials and courses on the topic.

When I began my real estate career there was very little material available on the negotiating subject, period. Over the next decade or so a few books of general interest appeared on the subject. But it's only been in the last ten years or so, that research has been done and case studies have been produced at the academic level.

Finally, some of our universities and professional schools are establishing faculties and departments that specialize in the field of negotiation. Because of the pioneering research done by Dr. Chester L. Karass and the experiments and papers produced on the subject as a result of work done at Harvard University and others, the subject has become intellectually fashionable.

In spite of all this however, one is still hard pressed to find anything on the subject that is directly related to real estate sales, and in particular to residential sales.

In the Chapters that follow you will find a wealth of negotiating information, strategies and street smart ideas that will enable you to get more appointments, write more listings, close more sales and earn more money selling real estate.

Naturally, every idea is not appropriate in every circumstance. Whether a technique is appropriate will depend on local laws and customs, as well as the type of representation a Salesperson has contracted to provide. After taking these matters into account, it will be up to the reader to determine whether using any idea contained in this book constitutes a proper practice.

Becoming a better negotiator is also a giant step towards managing your time more efficiently and effectively, so that as you earn more money you can have more time off with your family and loved ones, to enjoy the fruits of your labor. In fact, it's the shortest and most direct route to a successful real estate sales career.

If we want to become better at anything we do, the first step is to make some **decisions** to do things differently. If we want to become a better negotiator, then we have to convince the toughest party we ever negotiate with that change is necessary. The party I'm referring to is — ourselves. We're all products of the decisions we make in life, and our lives will only improve to the degree that we **decide**, to take the actions that are necessary to improve them. It's my hope that this book will cause its readers to make at least some decisions that will improve their lives.

Although this book is by no means the final word on real estate negotiating, it will help fill a void that is badly in need of filling. Hopefully it will be the catalyst for other aspiring and established authors alike, to make their contribution to a field that can certainly accommodate several more.

It's the author's intention to update and revise this publication on a regular basis. As a result, suggestions from readers, particularly those regarding areas that were not addressed in this edition will be welcomed.

Good Reading, Good Selling and Good Negotiating!

Marilyn Jennings,

c/o MCJ Publishing Ltd.
P.O. Box 6167, Stn. "A"
Calgary, Alberta, Canada T2H 2L4
Canada & USA Dial 1-800-736-2335
New Zealand   Dial 0-800-449-702
Australia   Dial 1-800-12-9096
                E-MAIL: office@mcjpub.com
                WEBSITE: www.mcjpub.com

TABLE
OF
CONTENTS

SECTION ONE

NEGOTIATING AND
REAL ESTATE SALES IN GENERAL

SECTION TWO

NEGOTIATING WITH SELLERS

S E C T I O N   T H R E E

NEGOTIATING WITH BUYERS

SECTION ONE

NEGOTIATING AND
REAL ESTATE SALES IN GENERAL

INTRODUCTION

Even as this book is being written, the real estate

industry is changing rapidly, and our role as negotiators is shifting widely from what it was a few short years ago. In fact many of those who have predeceased us would hardly recognize this business if they were around today.

Almost everywhere in North America, our legislatures and courts are rapidly redefining the agency relationships and fiduciary duties of real estate professionals. It can no longer be assumed that every salesperson involved in a real estate transaction automatically represents the Seller. No longer is every member of the local Real Estate Board or Multiple Listing Service automatically a Sub-agent of the Listing Broker. In most jurisdictions in North America, it's now mandatory for Real Estate Practitioners to disclose to Buyers and Sellers which side they represent. In some areas, new laws have been passed that seem to limit or alter the effects of the Common Law of Agency as it applies to real estate transactions. Where all these changes will ultimately lead us, only time will tell.

Not only are we living in an era where the rules and regulations by which we do business are changing rapidly, but we're living in an era that is ruled by advanced technology. The computer age is now! Its effects are here to stay! The real estate industry, like virtually every other industry, is being impacted more and more by computers every day. What an exciting time it is to be involved in real estate sales.

There is no longer any question that the economy of the future will be technology driven. The consumer is being conditioned more and more to expect information instantly, regarding every product that interests them. When the generations presently attending our educational institutions emerge as consumers, they'll be demanding even more information and will expect to receive it even faster. And this trend will continue. We better be prepared to provide instant answers to their questions, or we simply won't get our share of the consumer dollar. It's that simple!

The day is fast approaching when it will no longer be an option for every Real Estate Salesperson to have their own computer. It will be an absolute necessity! It will be impossible to remain competent without one.

To say this industry has a long way to go in this regard is an understatement. There are thousands of Salespeople out there who don't know the difference between a floppy disk and a cobweb, and have no intention of finding out. These people will not survive in this business much longer. In fact in many areas, large numbers of them have already become casualties of the technological revolution because they refused to change with the times.

There is no question that we're living in an era that requires us to learn to use new technology within the confines of new rules and regulations, on behalf of those we represent, in order to be successful. By all indications this process will continue in the foreseeable future. Eric Hoffer said, "In times of change, learners inherit the earth while the learned are often simply beautifully equipped to lead a world that no longer exists."

The evolution of new rules and regulations that will continue to redefine the role of the professional Real Estate Practitioner, coupled with the tremendous changes that new technology is bringing to the marketplace, means that Salespeople simply must become better negotiators.

To be a competent negotiator, the Real Estate Professional of the future will have to commit themselves to a program of continual learning, and to the use of the best technology available. If they are committed to anything less than this, it will be impossible for them to fulfill their duties and obligations to the Clients or Customers they represent.

In spite of all this, one fact remains unchanged — Real Estate Salespeople make their living by negotiating with others. Although we frequently find ourselves negotiating with other parties involved in the same transactions as we are, primarily the negotiations we undertake are with, and on behalf of Buyers and Sellers. That situation is not likely to change much in the future, except that our roles and who we represent will be more clearly defined.

There will always be a need for third party negotiators to represent Buyers and Sellers in real estate transactions and mediate differences between them. Abba Eban, the great Israeli statesman acknowledged the essential role that third party negotiators play between adversaries when he said, "It is a law of negotiation that each party can accept a compromise from a third party that it could never accept from its adversary or initiate itself."

So, no matter which party a Salesperson represents in a real estate transaction, whether it be the Buyers, or the Sellers, or if they're simply acting as a Mediator of sorts and representing neither or them, one thing is certain — the better a negotiator they become, the more successful they're going to be.

Therein lies the purpose of this book.

Good Reading and Good Negotiating!

CHAPTER 1

MOST IMPORTANT
SKILLS OF ALL

There are two old negotiating truisms that anyone

entering into negotiations of any kind ought to be aware of. The first one is, "He who speaks first loses". The second is, "The party who talks the most, gets the least".

SHUT UP
AND LISTEN

Contrary to what most people believe, when it comes to negotiating, it's far more important to be a good listener than to be a good talker! Most people go into negotiations so intent on covering points they want to make, they hardly hear anything anybody else says, until they have a chance to say their piece. When entering negotiations the best approach is to state your case as clearly and concisely as possible and then "shut up" and listen.

A
FORMIDABLE WEAPON

"Silence" is one of the most formidable weapons we have at our disposal when negotiating with others. Most people hate silence with a passion. Their natural instinct is to attempt to fill the void by talking. Every time this happens during the negotiating process, they provide you with reams of information, which is exactly what you want them to do. That's why it pays to listen carefully first, and let the other side do most of the talking.

By listening carefully instead of talking, you can pick up clues about what the other side really wants to accomplish. It's next to impossible for anyone to talk too long without giving something away. Studies have proven that almost invariably, the party who does the most talking makes the most concessions.

AT THE VERY
TOP OF THE LIST

To be an effective negotiator you have to master several basic skills. The most important skills of all are those that enable us to become a good listener. Research has proven beyond question that of all the skills demonstrated by leading negotiators, being a good listener is at the very top of the list. Nothing else even comes close in terms of importance.

If you want to become an effective negotiator, then it's absolutely vital that you become a good listener — that you master the skills of being able to do what I refer to as "Actual Listening". In fact, how good a listener you become, will determine your ultimate effectiveness as a negotiator.

SKILLS HAVE
TO BE LEARNED

Listening skills are not something we're born with. Like all of the skills we master in life, they have to be learned.

Without exception master negotiators will tell you, that the one set of skills they work daily at improving, are those associated with becoming a better listener. Because these skills are so vital to mastering the art of negotiating, it's necessary to work constantly at improving them. There are several ways we can do this.

LISTEN MORE
BY TALKING LESS

As we've already discussed you can improve your listening skills by minimizing the talking you do during a negotiating session. It's simply impossible to talk and listen at the same time. In addition, the more talking you do the more information you're likely to give away and the more outright concessions you're apt to make. If you're doing the giving there's little or no need for the other side to make concessions.

Over the years I've been involved in negotiations with other Salespeople and Brokers who did so much talking that my Client and I didn't have to make any concessions at all. There were all kinds of occasions on which we were willing to make concessions, but sadly we were never given the opportunity to do so.

LISTEN MORE
BY TAKING NOTES

Taking notes when the other side is talking is a great way of improving your listening skills, for all kinds of reasons. It keeps you from talking. It ensures you are paying close attention. It provides you with a record of what has been said. It eliminates the necessity of interrupting the other side prematurely to ask questions or make counterpoints because you might forget what was said. It flatters the ego of the other side and keeps them talking. It increases the odds the other side will give something away.

LISTEN MORE
BY ASKING QUESTIONS

Another way to improve your listening skills, is by showing a genuine interest in what the other side is saying. You can do this by politely asking questions about points you're not clear on when they've finished talking and it's your turn to speak. The best way to keep someone else talking till you get the information you want is to ask them questions in a friendly, nonthreatening manner. This strokes their ego and makes them feel important.

LISTEN MORE
BY NOT INTERRUPTING

Listening skills can be improved by not interrupting the other party when they're speaking, except in rare circumstances. There's really no need to interrupt someone when they're speaking, even to ask questions or clarify points, especially if you're taking notes.

Interruptions are discourteous and put the other side in a negative mindset. Research shows that people who frequently interrupt others usually make more concessions — perhaps because they haven't learned the art of being patient — another critical negotiating skill that we'll deal with later.

LISTEN MORE —
USE THE RSVQ FORMULA

You can sharpen your listening skills by Repeating, Summarizing, Verifying and Querying (the RSVQ formula) what the other side has said when it's your turn to talk. This is an important aspect of being a good listener. It helps avoid misunderstandings and confusion over the issues in question.

If the other side has been unclear on some points, or if you have any doubt as to what they said, ask them to repeat the statements. From time to time, summarize your understanding of the progress being made. Then ask them to verify your interpretation of what has been said. Query the meaning of key terms, so you know there's no misunderstanding as you proceed. Using the RSVQ formula as negotiations progress, will confirm your understanding of their position as they restate it. It will also obtain closure on points as they're dealt with.

Using the RSVQ formula also ensures that one party doesn't assume an issue has been settled, while the other side believes it's still negotiable. Never assume the other party has exactly the same understanding of key issues and terms that you have. Who gets the interest in the deposit cheque between now and closing? If there's any doubt get it clarified during the negotiations — not afterwards!

LISTEN MORE
WITH EYE CONTACT

One of the best ways to improve your listening skills is to ensure you have frequent eye contact with the other party when they are speaking. Conversely, if you want to ensure the other party hears what you say when it's your turn to speak, maintain frequent eye contact with them. Frequent eye contact is considered to be one of the key elements in effective communicating.

When your eyes meet those of another party who is speaking to you, and you maintain that eye contact for a minimum of 5 to 10 seconds at a time, two things happen. You connect with that person, and he connects with you. He gets his point across and you hear what he's saying. You can then deal effectively with his concerns and objections.

FOUNDATION FOR
EFFECTIVE NEGOTIATING

As stated earlier in this chapter, our effectiveness as negotiators will be directly proportionate to how completely we develop our listening skills.

The relationship between being an effective negotiator and being a good listener is the same as that of a building to its foundation. Good listening skills provide the foundation for effective negotiating. Until a person understands the importance of developing and continually honing their listening skills, any examination of the negotiating issue would be of little value. Mindful of this fact, we'll proceed to Chapter 2.

CHAPTER 2

A
NEGOTIATING VIRTUE

In addition to being a good listener, which we dealt

with in the previous chapter, there are a number of other skills, that are of paramount importance and must also be mastered if you want to become an effective negotiator. The more impatient you are, the more difficult it is to be a good listener. In fact if you're really impatient it's virtually impossible to be a good listener.

Patience is always a virtue, but it's even more so when you're involved in negotiations than in almost any other facet of life. Research has shown that patient negotiators are generally more successful, particularly when they're dealing with impatient people on the other side.

REAL ESTATE
AGENTS OFTEN LOSE

Real Estate Agents often lose because they're impatient negotiators. Rather than learning to negotiate properly and let the Seller and Buyer come to terms, Salespeople themselves often become a commodity in the negotiating process. They allow themselves to be manipulated by Buyers and Sellers almost at will.

While presenting offers with other Agents, I've been put on the spot in front of both my Sellers and theirs, about throwing in part of my commission, practically before we got seated at the table.

I've also been asked to purchase, or share in the purchase of: stoves, fridges, freezers, TVs, satellite dishes, washers, dryers, broadloom, drapes, curtains and literally anything else you could name.

A
POWERFUL ALLY

When asked to cut my commission or share in the purchase of any item my answer is always the same. An unqualified "No"! And when I say "No", I mean No! This little two letter word can be one of the most powerful allies a Salesperson ever had, if they use it correctly when they're asked to cut their commission.

The next time you're presenting an offer on another Agents' listing and you get asked by the Seller or the other Agent to cut your commission try this. Just say "No". Don't say anything else. Simply say "No" and shut up. There's no need to explain!

IT'S NOT
DEBATABLE

When you proffer an explanation you immediately weaken your position, because you're tendering information that's debatable. However when you say "No" and don't attempt to explain, it's definite. It's not debatable. It puts the other side in a difficult position. They don't know how to deal with the situation.

I've done this for years. As I look them square in the eye, I simply say, "No". Then I shut up — and watch! Usually the person asking the question gets badly embarrassed. They get red in the face. They squirm in their chair. Then to save face they quickly change the subject to something more appropriate.

LIKE
EATING POPCORN

There isn't a more effective way of lowering the expectations of the other side than by refusing to cut your commission. It sends a clear message that you are in control; that your paycheck is not a commodity available to everyone involved in the negotiations. Cutting commissions is like eating popcorn — once you start it's hard to stop.

WE PAY FOR ONE;
YOU DO ONE FREE

I let one deal die because I refused to cut my commission as little as $250. The case I'm referring to involved a local financial institution during a nasty recession. The principle they operated on was — We Pay For One; You Do One Free. It's an idea that's been around for a long time. It's used by a lot of Sellers to get Real Estate Agents to work for less than they're worth. Unfortunately, a large number of Salespeople don't recognize it for what it really is. They don't understand how it works to their detriment.

That particular institution was dealing with all kinds of Salespeople. They were able to get most of them to give up as much as 50% of their commission on offers they brought them on their foreclosed properties. They operated that way until all their foreclosures were sold.

EVERY SECOND
DEAL WAS FREE

I probably sold more of this financial institution's properties than any of the other Agents. I got paid my full commission on every one. Other salespeople were always telling me how they hated getting offers on that institution's listings, because they got beaten out of half their commission on every deal.

When asked why they didn't blow one on the institution like I did to make my point, they said they were afraid of losing a deal. The truth of the matter was, they were too impatient to go through a proper negotiating process.

The fact is they lost a lot more by doing the deal for half, than they would have lost by not doing it at all. Every second deal they did with that institution, they were doing totally free — without earning a nickel for their efforts. They got paid for one; they did one free.

If I'd asked those same Agents if they were willing to do every second deal for every Client without charging a commission, they'd have asked me what I was smoking. Yet that's exactly what they got manipulated into doing without realizing it.

EVEN WORSE
IF AN INDIVIDUAL

If the Seller was an individual rather than an institution the result would have been even worse. On every deal the Salesperson did with that Seller in the future, the Seller would expect the same treatment on commission.

On top of that, everyone else the Seller referred to that Agent, would expect the same treatment. The cycle would then continue because the next generation of referrals would expect the same treatment. Forever and a day, for every two deals that Salesperson did with that Seller or his friends, or friends of his friends, he'd get paid for only one.

THE BIG
PICTURE

Being patient allows you to understand the big picture, analyze key issues better; understand the goals of the other side; evaluate trade-offs; and test the strengths and weaknesses of the other side.

Being patient means taking the time to determine if it makes sense to become involved in the transaction in the first place. If you frequently find yourself giving up part of your commission, or paying for appliances or other items in order to put deals together, then you haven't learned the art or the value of being a patient negotiator.

It's a fact that impatient salespeople spend much of their time on transactions that provide them a relatively low return for their efforts. Conversely, salespeople who have mastered the art of being patient, spend their time working on transactions that reward them lavishly. That's because patient salespeople have taken the time to analyze the Big Picture. They realize it makes sense to turn down deals on which they are unable to negotiate a proper paycheck for themselves.

Being patient — maintaining your position as long as possible without giving in — and providing evidence to support your position, eventually lowers the expectations of the other side. Being patient provides time to work out a mutually beneficial agreement, and provides a Salesperson with the confidence to say "No" if that's not possible.

ESSENCE OF
TRUE NEGOTIATION

Patience is the catalyst that brings the negotiating process back to life when it seems to be faltering. Being patient and thinking things through, drastically reduces the possibility of making unnecessary concessions that don't accomplish the objectives you want them to. When both sides to negotiations exercise self-restraint, any agreement they reach will generally be more beneficial to each of them. Patience is the essence of true negotiation. As such it will be referred to often throughout this book.

C H A P T E R   3

NICE GUYS
FINISH FIRST

Among the qualities demonstrated by effective negotiators, being a "Nice Guy" is right up there with being a good listener and being patient. Research proves that nice guys finish first, when it comes to negotiating.

A RADICAL DIGRESSION

This seems like a perfect spot to digress for a moment and address an item I'll have to cope with after this book is published. I've used the term "nice guys" throughout this chapter and the words "him" and "his" to describe Buyers, Sellers, other Real Estate Salespeople and Brokers elsewhere throughout this book. Because of this there's little doubt I'll receive more than a few letters and phone calls from radical feminists and those preoccupied with the political correctness issue who happen to read it.

I'm not into radical feminism or political correctness. I have no intention of getting involved in satisfying either element. I hope that anyone inclined towards converting me, will expend their energy, time and money on something more likely to bear them results.

I've been able to accomplish every goal I set out to accomplish in life so far. Along the way I've received advice and support from countless members of both sexes. That's not to say that women have existed in a perfect world. Far from it. There were inequities that needed to be rectified. There still are and there always will be. On the other hand, it's not a perfect world for everyone who is a member of the male gender either.

I do applaud and support wholeheartedly, those women and men who've made it their objective to take the high road, and work together in a positive manner, towards eliminating inequities that have crept into society which are grossly unfair to women or any other segment of the population.

MY GENDER IS IRRELEVANT

I believe it's my primary responsibility in life to be a decent human being, and that my gender which is the result of an accident of birth, is totally irrelevant. My role models in life have been members of both genders. They've been people of genuine character and real accomplishment such as Abraham Lincoln, Helen Keller, Justice Thurgood Marshall, Thomas Bata, Mother Teresa, Dr. Napoleon Hill, Golda Meir, Dr. Robert Shuller and Lady Margaret Thatcher.

These are all people of great achievement who have led exemplary and principled lives; who in spite of having to overcome great adversity, rose to the top in their chosen fields. To them being male or female wasn't important. What was important first and foremost was being a first class, decent human being.

MALE CONSPIRACY?

If I subscribed to the theory that all the difficulties women experience getting ahead in life are the result of some male conspiracy, I'd have given up before I even came close to reaching the goals I've achieved in life. I can't help but wonder how many women have accomplished far less in life than they would otherwise have done, if they hadn't been influenced negatively by the radical feminists.

I'LL BE A NICE GUY
TILL THE DAY I DIE

As for political correctness, I've been a "Nice Guy" for years. I can't for the life of me see how mankind, or womankind or humankind or anykind or everykind for that matter, will be any worse off if I continue to be a "Nice Guy" till the day I die. I'm sure you get the point.

In any case I've digressed enough already, so let's get back to discussing "Nice Guys" in the negotiating sense which is far more important and meaningful.

NICE GUYS
GIVE UP LESS

During negotiations "Nice Guys" are always polite, considerate and good mannered. They don't contradict the other side abruptly. They avoid expressions of fixed opinion. They don't make proclamations that the opinions of the other side are "a bunch of lies" or that they are "ridiculous".

Nice guys sympathize with the needs and desires of the other side. They are sincerely regretful when they have to take a conflicting position, but they take it and stick to it when they have to, without being belligerent or offensive.

Research has shown that when negotiations reach a point where someone has to make a concession in order to reach an agreement, negotiators who are "Nice Guys" will likely have to give up less than those who are not.

A LESSON
FROM BEN FRANKLIN

I don't know of anything that makes a better case for being a "Nice Guy", than these few paragraphs from the autobiography of Benjamin Franklin, who in addition to being a great statesman was regarded as one of the best negotiators who ever lived, and I quote:

> *"I made it a rule to forbear all direct contra-*
> *dictions to the sentiments of others, and all*
> *positive assertions of my own. I even forbade*
> *myself the use of every word or expression in the*
> *language that imported a "fixed opinion", such*
> *as "certainly", "undoubtedly", etc. I adopted*
> *instead of them, "I conceive", "I apprehend", or*
> *"I imagine" a thing to be so and so; or "So it*
> *appears to me at present".*

> *When another asserted something that I*
> *thought an error, I denied myself the pleasure of*
> *contradicting him abruptly, and of showing*
> *immediately some absurdity in his proposition. In*
> *answering I began by observing that in certain*
> *circumstances his opinion would be right, but in*
> *the present case there appeared or seemed to me*
> *some other difference, etc.*

> *I soon found the advantage of this change in*
> *my manner; the conversations I engaged in went*
> *more pleasantly. The modest way in which I pro-*

posed my opinions procured them a readier reception and less contradiction. I had less mortification when I was found to be in the wrong, and I more easily prevailed with others to give up their mistakes and join with me when I happened to be in the right" .

ASK
NICE QUESTIONS

It's a good idea then, to get in the habit of asking nice questions, rather than stating definite and contradictory opinions. Here's a few examples:

1) "Do you really think that's fair?" instead of, "That's unfair."

2) "Have you considered doing it this way?" instead of, "That's not the way to do it at all."

3) "If you were in my Buyer's shoes and had three other homes to choose from which are almost as suitable as yours, would you think it fair if I brought you a counter-offer like your proposing here?" instead of, "My Buyer will never go for that."

4) "Why take a chance on blowing the deal when we're this close?" instead of, "That'll blow the deal for sure."

5) "Can I make a suggestion?" instead of, "This is the only way to do it."

A
MAGIC WORD

I should mention here that the word "Fair", which was used in a couple of the previous questions, can be a magic word when used in negotiations. Everybody likes to think they're a "Fair" individual.

When someone is being unreasonable, I can usually make them squirm in their chair and rethink their position, by looking them straight in the eye and asking my favorite **Nice Guy** question, "Do you really think that's fair?"

CHAPTER 4

TWO FORMS
OF NEGOTIATING

Basically there are only two forms of negotiating. One

form is "adversary" negotiating. With this form of negotiating one side wins and the other side loses. This is the form of negotiating that often takes place when lawyers or attorneys become involved in the process.

Attorneys have been trained to believe that whenever there are conflicting positions, sides have to be formed. One side will win and the other side will lose. They believe their Clients need to be protected so they don't end up on the losing side. They've been taught that the best way to look after their Clients is to fight for them.

A
DECLARATION OF WAR

Quite often when attorneys become involved in the negotiating process, the first step they take is what amounts to a declaration of war on the other side. On many occasions individuals approach an attorney to prepare a simple agreement that reflects the outcome of collaborative efforts they undertook to negotiate an acceptable solution to a problem, only to find themselves instantly involved in a complex adversarial situation.

To be fair it should be pointed out that on occasion, by the time attorneys get involved in the negotiating process the parties they represent are already true adversaries in their own right. But it's a rare occurrence when an attorney focuses his efforts on finding a solution that works for everyone involved as opposed to winning the war.

What we have to remember with this form of negotiating is that whenever there is both a winner and a loser, in the end there's at least one unhappy party. This form of negotiating can best be described as "Win-Lose" negotiating. And at its ugly worst it's truly "Lose-Lose" negotiating.

In many cases even the so-called winners lose because the negotiations drag on for ages and cost an absolute fortune in legal fees, to say nothing of the worry, mental stress and negative psychological impact on their lives. The fact is, adversary negotiations often fail to produce a winner at all and everybody involved in the process loses — except the attorneys.

IDEAL FOR
REAL ESTATE

The other form of negotiating is "collaborative" negotiating. With this form of negotiating, both sides concentrate on solving problems in a way that's beneficial to all. I like to refer to this form of negotiating as "Win-Win" negotiating. All sides win and nobody loses. Since the real estate business is so service intensive and people oriented, this form of negotiating is ideal and far more profitable for all of the parties involved.

NEGOTIATORS!
WHO ARE THEY ANYWAY?

When we think of negotiators, the first thing that comes to mind are those glamorous types we see on television, hear about on radio and read about in newspapers all the time. We're all familiar with those high profile mediators appointed by governments to intervene in and settle labor disputes that threaten the economy. We also hear and read about the high-powered negotiators who work out corporate mergers and takeovers. Then there are the diplomatic types who carry out ongoing negotiations between governments, concerning any number of vital issues that drastically affect our lives — issues such as taxes and trade, war and peace, and so on.

The fact is however, these high profile types are involved in but a tiny fraction of the total negotiations that take place daily all over the world. The majority of negotiations take place between ordinary individuals as they go about their daily business. How successful these individuals are in life, is determined to a large degree, by how skillful they are at conducting the negotiations they undertake.

MOST DIRECT
ROUTE TO SUCCESS

As Real Estate Salespeople we often forget that a major part of our time is spent negotiating in one way or another. Like those in other walks of life, the better negotiators we become — the more negotiating techniques we can master — the more successful we'll be at our jobs.

In fact, becoming a better negotiator is the easiest and most direct approach to getting more appointments, writing more listings and closing more sales. In addition, it's a giant step towards managing your time more efficiently and effectively, so you can have more time with your family and loved ones to enjoy the fruits of your labor. It's the shortest and most direct route to success.

BETTER NEGOTIATORS
ARE MORE SUCCESSFUL

In the real estate business we start the negotiating process the minute we begin dealing with a prospect. We negotiate an appointment time to meet for a Buyer Interview, to sign a Buyer Agency Agreement or to do a Listing Presentation. Did you ever wonder why some Real Estate Salespeople you know get more appointments from the calls they make or from calls they receive than others do? The answer is simple. These Salespeople are simply better negotiators than those whose average is lower.

We persuade people to list their homes with us; to make offers; to accept offers; to make counter-offers and to accept counter-offers.When we convince someone to list their home with us we negotiate the commission we charge; we negotiate bonuses on our listings and we negotiate the expiry dates on our listings. And when we convince Buyers to sign a Buyer Agency Agreement and hire us to represent them in their home purchase, we negotiate the retainer and fee we're going to charge for our services.

The fact of the matter is, Salespeople who enjoy a better batting average in all these aspects of the real estate business, are simply better negotiators than those with poorer averages. The better we get at negotiating these items the more we're going to sell; the more money we're going to make; the more time we'll be able to take off and the more successful we're going to be.

REASON FOR HIGH
INDUSTRY TURNOVER

From some of the experiences I've had and I'm sure

many of you as well, we not only have to negotiate our commission with the Seller when we take a listing. We often have to negotiate our commission with other Salespeople too, when they decide during an Offer Presentation that we should both work for less than we're worth in order to put a deal together.

Although this shouldn't happen at all, it does occur far too often. It's merely a symptom of the poor job our industry does when it comes to teaching Real Estate Salespeople how to become good negotiators. As I stated earlier in the Preface, the last thing we teach licensees in this industry, if we teach it to them at all, is how to make a living. Whether we want to admit it or not, that's one of the main reasons why the turnover in our industry is so outrageously high.

As we proceed through the following Chapters we'll discuss a variety of techniques that will enable you to become a better negotiator in all these aspects of real estate sales.

CHAPTER 5

A WORD
ABOUT CONCESSIONS

The proper "exchange" of concessions is considered

to be one of the most important techniques in effective negotiating.

And notice we said the "exchange" of concessions. Research proves that when you "exchange" concessions you win, because you get something in return for what you give up. On the other hand when you "make" or "give" outright concessions you lose, because you get nothing in return.

So to avoid the pitfall of making outright concessions, it's vitally important we learn to think in terms of "exchanging" concessions, as opposed to "making" or "giving" concessions.

ALWAYS GET
SOMETHING IN RETURN

Never, under any circumstances make or give "good-will concessions". Always be sure you get something in return for anything you give up. And always try to get something of equal or greater value than what you're giving up.

First of all the other side will always accept anything you give them for nothing. Secondly, "goodwill concessions" usually have the opposite effect. They appear as a sign of weakness and raise the expectations of the other side.

WHAT HAVE
THEY GOT TO LOSE

Another reason for not giving "goodwill concessions"

is, they usually prolong negotiations. After all, if the other side gets one concession easily without having to give anything up in exchange, what have they got to lose by prolonging the negotiations to see what else you might give up on the same basis. In other words, making or giving goodwill concessions encourages the other side to wait you out.

The same thing applies if you're impatient and make concessions that are too large, and if you give concessions too frequently. Experienced negotiators recommend that if you have to make more than one concession, each subsequent concession should be smaller than the previous one.

TIMING IS
IMPORTANT

Timing is also really important when making concessions. Again research shows that the first party to make a major concession usually comes out worse off in the final settlement. That's one reason why it pays to be patient and wait the other side out.

Before you make a concession use a little "sell". Make sure the other side sees the value in it. Point out what it's worth and think out loud what it will cost, and how much it will inconvenience both you and your Client or Customer. And remember that people don't place much value on things they get too easily.

CHAPTER 6

NEGOTIATING TO WIN
OR NEGOTIATING TO LOSE

When you make a concession and get something of

equal or greater value in return — that's negotiating to win. When you make a concession and get nothing in exchange, or you give up more than the value of the concession without realizing it — that's negotiating to lose. The important thing to realize is that people place different values on things. Because of this, both parties to a negotiation can make concessions and both can get something of greater value than they give up. That's what "Win-Win" negotiating is all about.

It's a pretty basic concept with some pretty basic economic consequences. If we trade for more, our standard of living improves. If we trade even, our standard of living more or less stays the same. If we trade for less, our standard of living declines.

THE
APPLIANCE PURCHASE

Some time ago I got a call from a Real Estate Salesperson I've known for a long time. He came to me for a personal consultation because his income was way down from previous years. I still find the story hard to believe.

He told me that earlier that year while negotiating a deal he'd bought the Buyer a fridge, stove, and dishwasher. Since then he was spending a lot of time and money at the Appliance Warehouse; buying fridges, stoves, and dishwashers for a number of other Buyers who were referred to him by the original Buyer, his friends, friends of theirs and so on.

He was caught up in a chain reaction that started with the original Buyer on whose transaction he made very little money after deducting the cost of the appliances.

Since then he'd bought appliances for so many people that now, nearly everyone he dealt with was expecting a set of appliances if they bought through him.

He said he felt like he was being carried downstream by a strong current even though he was swimming upstream as fast as he could. He was doing more deals and was working a lot harder than he ever had before. Yet he was earning far less money for his efforts. He wanted to know how to get out of that rut. He paid me for a couple of hours of my time to tell him how. We spent a good part of the time talking about negotiating to win rather than negotiating to lose.

He was involved in a trend that sees more and more Real Estate Salespeople making commission concessions to both Buyers and Sellers and then end up working for less than their expenses. He'd finally realized that buying appliances for Clients is a little bit like eating popcorn — once you start it's hard to stop.

I pointed out that he should be thankful he recognized the problem before it was too late; that a large number of Salespeople leave this business every year because they fail to learn one simple lesson — that when you make commission concessions during the negotiating process everybody wins but you.

"FROST-FREE FREDDY"

I told him the story about "Frost-Free Freddy", a Salesperson who had an offer on one of my listings some time ago. My driver nicknamed him "Frost-Free Freddy" and we've referred to him that way ever since. The reason for the nickname will soon become obvious.

After hearing the "Frost-Free Freddy" story, my friend got out of the appliance business, went back to doing things properly, and is now doing better than ever selling real estate.

IMPATIENT
NO-CLASS ACT

"Frost-Free" was on a 50/50 split with his company, so his half of the commission should have been $1975 based on what the property sold for. When he presented his offer he informed us that his Buyer couldn't go a nickel higher. He told us he agreed to buy them a frost-free refrigerator just to get the offer, and this cost him $750. Theoretically he still stood to make $1225 if the deal went together.

My Seller signed the offer back $1500 higher. In front of my Seller this impatient no-class act, suggested I throw in $750 and he'd throw in $750 and the deal would be done. I explained that my contribution to his Buyers' home purchase would be zero, and not a penny more — that I don't cut commission for anyone and my Seller was already aware of that.

HE WAS
TRUE TO HIS WORD

One thing I've learned over the years is that if nothing else, the "Frost-Free Freddies" of this world are scrupulous about keeping their word. After he left, I mentioned this fact to my Seller. I pointed out he was going to get at least half of what he'd countered the offer for, because "Frost-Free" already said he was willing to cut his commission at least that much more.

Before long he returned with a counter-offer that made me look like a genius to my Seller. Using another chunk of "Frost-Free's" commission the Buyer offered to split the difference. True to his word, good old "Frost-Free" threw in the $750 just like he said he'd do.

WILLING TO
BUY HIM A HOUSE

He informed us once more that the Buyer wouldn't budge a penny. I mean — why would he? I'm sure he couldn't believe his good fortune! He'd probably never seen a windfall like this in his life! Why, good old "Frost-Free" who he'd just met a few days ago, was actually willing to buy him a house!

At this point we were still $750 apart and "Frost-Free" had only $475 left to bargain away. My Seller who by now was really learning fast, did the smart thing. He countered for an additional $375, in effect splitting the difference once again.

At this point our impatient all-star negotiator suggested I should throw in the $375, since he'd already thrown in $1500, and he knew for sure his Buyer wouldn't come up at all.

I informed him once more that I wasn't prepared to make any contribution at all — that my contribution to his Buyer's home purchase would be exactly zero, and not a penny more. So off he went again to see his Buyer. He phoned in about 10 minutes to say we had a deal; that he threw in the other $375 and he'd deliver the copies to me in the morning.

When he delivered the copies to me the next morning, he took another shot at trying to get me to participate in his commission cutting binge. Needless to say he was unsuccessful once again, and he left my office all upset and calling me a cheapskate.

PATIENCE GENERATES PROFITS

Let's take a look at what happened here. "Frost-Free Freddy" made a lousy $100 for a few days work and has since left the business. I made my full commission because I had enough patience to wait the silly fool out.

Folks, we're supposed to be in a business! One of the main objectives of being in business is to generate a profit, so both ourselves and our families can enjoy a better standard of living. And we'll be much more successful at generating profits if we learn to become patient negotiators!

AN IMPORTANT LESSON

Isn't it interesting that absolutely everybody was a winner here except poor old "Frost-Free Freddy"? The Seller was a winner. The Buyer was a winner. I was a winner. There's a very important lesson to be learned from all this. That lesson is this: **"When you cut your commission — everyone wins but you"**!

ABSOLUTE WORST
THING YOU CAN DO

The absolute worst thing you can do is agree to cut your commission when doing a Listing Presentation. The immediate result is you lose the Seller's respect and confidence. From that moment on the Seller is in control. He'll be on your case, calling the shots every step of the way. Every day he'll be making demands on your time and telling you how to do your job. If you want to get to really hate this business and drive yourself bonkers in no time, just agree to cut your commission on the next several listings you take.

When a Seller tells me he'll only give me the listing if I'll take it at a reduced amount because another Salesperson is willing to do that, I simply apply the techniques outlined in Chapter 13. After using these approaches no one ever wants to list for less.

Commission cutters are Real Estate Salespeople and Brokers who have nothing else to offer! They're actually on their way out of the business although they don't know it yet. They're one of the plagues of the real estate business that I wish I didn't have to contend with. In all my years in the business I've never found it necessary to cut a commission. Purchasing appliances or cutting commission in any form is like eating popcorn — once you start it's hard to stop! Before long everyone you deal with will expect the same concession from you. The best approach is not to start.

THE FRIENDS
AND RELATIVES SYNDROME

When it comes to the commission issue, there's one

mysterious aspect about our business that I've never been able to understand. Why is it that when a person gets a Real Estate License they seem to acquire almost immediately what I refer to as "The Friends and Relatives Syndrome".

I've made it a policy over the years, that I never contribute my expertise as a Real Estate Professional to anybody unless they pay for it. I don't cut my commission for anyone. Not for friends. Not for relatives. Not for anyone. Period!

It has always puzzled me that so many Salespeople feel obligated to provide their services free or at drastically reduced rates to friends and relatives. At my Mini-Rallies® Salespeople often complain about this problem. They ask me how I cope with it. When I answer that it's a problem I've never had to contend with they're mystified. The only explanation they give for having to deal with the problem themselves is that their friends and relatives expect it.

When I ask them if they do anything to **encourage** the situation they usually say no. The interesting thing is that when I ask them if they do anything to **discourage** the situation they also answer no.

In any case, I find it difficult to believe that their friends and relatives automatically expected that once the Salesperson got their Real Estate License, they'd do all their friends' and relatives' real estate deals for little or nothing.

I can't for the life of me understand why relatives or friends would expect me to give up my commission to sell their home. That's how I spend my time. That's how I earn my living! They know I don't expect them to forego any of their time at work, to contribute to my livelihood. Why in heaven's name should they expect it from me?

If we want to get the maximum return on the money, the time and the effort we invest in this business, it's crucial that we become expert at negotiating better paychecks for ourselves. We have to learn how to negotiate for the maximum rather than the minimum. In Chapter 13 we'll discuss how you can ensure this happens on every listing you write.

CHAPTER 7

SOURCES OF
NEGOTIATING POWER

Among a variety of sources that give us power as

negotiators are such things as influence, reputation, attitude, commitment, time and knowledge. There are others but they don't apply as directly to real estate sales as these do. The interesting thing is that all of these have to be either "earned" or "learned". In other words if you want to become a more effective negotiator, you have to work constantly at developing these sources of power for yourself. If you work constantly at developing these sources of power for yourself, your effectiveness as a negotiator will continue to improve.

INFLUENCE = NEGOTIATING POWER

First of all there's influence and influence is born out of respect. When you earn the respect of another, you have influence with that person as well as with other people that person knows.

The best way to maximize the "influence" you have in your marketing area, is to build "client-for-life relationships" and win the "respect" of everyone you deal with. Unless you win the respect of the Buyers and Sellers you deal with, you'll have no influence with them, and as a result you won't receive repeat business or referrals from them.

On the other hand, the greater the respect your Clients have for you, the more influence you'll have with them and the more comfortable they'll feel about referring others to you.

By the same token, the greater the respect you have with other Realtors, both locally and from other communities, the more influence you'll have with them and the more Realtor referrals you'll receive from them as well.

Think about this for a minute. Next to repeat clients themselves, prospects referred to you by your Clients or your peers in the business, are the easiest people in the world to deal with. Because of the influence you have with the party referring them to you, they'll trust you implicity before they even meet you.

The same thing applies when you refer one of your Clients to another Realtor. Because of the influence you have with your Client, the Realtor receiving the referral will enjoy immediate respect and influence with the Client, that he'd never enjoy with a cold prospect.

There's simply no question about it; being in a position to influence someone else, provides you with an indisputable source of power in the negotiating process.

REPUTATION = NEGOTIATING POWER

Reputation is another major source of negotiating power, and the key to developing a good reputation is building trust. In fact, collaborative negotiations simply can't succeed without mutual trust.

The best way to build trust is to do business fairly, honestly and straightforwardly with every person you deal with; your Sellers; your Buyers; your peers in the business; and with those not in the business that you deal with frequently, such as appraisers; home inspectors; mortgage people; lawyers and so on.

Isn't a Realtor with a "solid reputation" for being honest and giving good service, in a more powerful position when negotiating deals, than someone who has a poor reputation? The answer is obvious, isn't it!

So if you want to become a more powerful negotiator it's vital that you work constantly at developing and strengthening your reputation both inside and outside the real estate industry.

ATTITUDE = NEGOTIATING POWER

Research proves that a Salesperson will be a far more effective negotiator if he is solidly committed to achieving specific objectives and goals for himself and his family. When committed in this way the Salesperson is far more likely to enter negotiations with a positive attitude about the outcome.

If you're going to succeed at any negotiating session it's absolutely vital that you have a positive mental attitude about the task at hand. You "gotta believe" that your goal is not only justifiable but also attainable. You may enter negotiations with high hopes and the best of intentions, but for sure you will not succeed if the other side senses they are more committed to their position than you are to yours.

Since there are situations when you don't have much time to develop an atmosphere of trust, such as when you go to present an offer on someone else's listing, your attitude can dictate the success or failure of a negotiation. If you demonstrate by your words and actions that you are confident and fair, honest and trustworthy, people will always place their faith in you.

On the other hand if you appear unconfident and suspicious of people, they'll be wary of you. In fact if you come across that way Sellers will regard you as the enemy. However if you come across confidently they'll regard you as their ally — everytime!! Take control at the beginning of a negotiating session and set the tone by being positive and friendly, instead of being threatening and intimidating.

COMMITMENT = NEGOTIATING POWER

Research also proves that commitment is one of the main sources of power a Salesperson can have at his disposal when it comes to being a successful negotiator. And commitment takes several forms.

First of all there's the Salesperson's commitment to his company. The stronger his commitment to his company, its products, its business practices and its philosophy — the more effective a negotiator he'll be.

Then there's the company's commitment to him. And just like his commitment to the company, the stronger their commitment is to him — the more effective a negotiator he'll be.

Research also proves that the more evident this commitment is to the public the greater will be its impact on negotiations. That's why the awards programs sponsored by both the real estate industry and by real estate companies are so important. They're one of the most effective ways of demonstrating mutual commitment to the public.

Think about this for example! If a Salesperson has been with his company for a long time, and he receives recognition awards from both his company and his industry on a regular basis, doesn't this give him added negotiating power when competing with others? The answer is obvious isn't it!!

So if you want to gain a bundle of negotiating power over your competition, one of the most effective ways to accomplish this is to get involved in winning as many of your company and industry awards as you possibly can.

LETTERS OF RECOMMENDATION

Similarly, the stronger a Salesperson's commitment is to his Clients, and the stronger their commitment is to him — the more effective a negotiator he'll be. What about the Salesperson who has letters of recommendation from almost every Client he's ever dealt with? Doesn't this give him additional negotiating power with prospects, Clients and competitors alike? Again the answer is obvious, isn't it?

Let me make a point here about letters of recommendation from Clients, because very few Salespeople from any field of sales for that matter, understand their real significance. Letters of recommendation aren't really letters of recommendation at all!! **What they really are is this: they're letters of commitment — from your Client to you!!**

One of the questions most frequently asked by Salespeople at my Mini-Rallies® is, "What do I do with all these letters of recommendation from Clients after I get them?" They can be used for a variety of purposes. Use them in ads, brochures, resumes and other literature to promote yourself personally. Use them as references with both Buyers and Sellers to convince them to deal with you. Use them to prove your goodwill when you retire and sell your business to another Salesperson. The list is endless.

However, what you do with these letters is really not the important thing here. The whole point of the exercise is to get your Clients committed to you in writing!

Just think about it! When someone puts their opinion in writing they're committed to it! They'll stand behind it!! They'll defend it vigorously!!! They'll pass it on to just about everybody they know!!!!

So once again, if you want to gain some real negotiating power over your competition, and at the same time get your Clients firmly committed to you, then solicit letters of recommendation from every Client you deal with from now on!! And get letters of recommendation from all your past Clients as well!!!

TIME =
<u>NEGOTIATING POWER</u>

Time is another major source of negotiating power for Salespeople who learn to use it properly.

We've all heard that old expression — time is money! That statement is truer in negotiating than in any other aspect of life, but in a context totally different from the way Salespeople normally interpret its meaning.

When it comes to negotiating, "The more time you take — the more money you make". There's an old proverb that says, "Take time from the urgent to do what's important". That's crucial advice for any Real Estate Salesperson wanting to become an effective negotiator.

One of the most essential qualities demonstrated by expert negotiators is the art of being patient which we dealt with in Chapter 2 at the beginning of this book. But it's important to note here, that it's impossible to be patient if you're always in a rush.

We've got to teach Salespeople in this business to slow down and smell the roses. Being in a hurry costs them a fortune. One after another throughout my career, I've seen Salespeople leave thousands and thousands of dollars on the table, simply because they didn't take the time to find out what we were willing to give up.

They rushed in and cut their commission to put the deal together. In the process they left the difference between a profitable and an unprofitable deal, for themselves and their families on the table. And the same thing happens over and over again, when Salespeople are competing with one another for listings.

ALWAYS
IN A RUSH

Real Estate Salespeople are always in a rush. That's how we train them. We're notorious in this industry for conditioning new Salespeople into believing that it's virtually impossible for anyone selling real estate for a living to lead a balanced family life. I've seen perfectly sane people come into this business from other walks of life, and in a matter of days an amazing transformation takes place.

The first thing that happens is we get them 500 business cards that say — guess what? They can be reached at a certain telephone number 24 hours a day. By the time a couple of weeks go by we've convinced them that not only is this a 24 hour a day business, but by golly they've got to do it all by themselves.

Guess what happens next? Why we send these poor souls down to get a pager. From that date onwards they begin serving a "life sentence" where they're totally controlled by a silly beeper. They don't even get time off for good behavior!

A COUPLE
OF SUGGESTIONS

If you want to get some balance in your life, I've got a couple of suggestions for you that really worked for me. First of all check your business cards and other printed material. If the words "24 Hours" appear on them anywhere, throw them away and get new ones without that on them. If you want your life to be normal the last thing you need, is to be constantly reading and brainwashing yourself into believing you're in a 24 hour-a-day business.

And the absolute best bit of advice I can give to any licenced Real Estate Salesperson is if you carry a pager — get rid of it. It wasn't until I obtained my freedom from the beeper by getting rid of it, that my life became normal again. One after another Clients, friends and family members began telling me how much more they enjoyed being with me, and how rudely they felt I'd been treating them when I carried that silly thing.

PEOPLE ARE
NOT IMPRESSED

I can tell you from personal experience, that people are not impressed when there's a pager beeping and vibrating constantly while you're dealing with them. Not only do they consider it rude and distracting, but it keeps us constantly on edge and interferes with our ability to concentrate on whatever important matter we're dealing with at the time.

But worse than anything else, Salespeople get up in the morning with a fantastic plan to do all these "income producing activities" during the day — a plan that would make them nothing but money. Then the pager starts beeping. Before you know it they've spent the whole day re-acting to one page after another and they've accomplished nothing "income producing" at all.

How in heaven's name can we expect our lives to be normal if we continually subject both ourselves and those we care about to this kind of abuse.

After I got rid of the pager I came to realize, that contrary to what I'd been taught, nothing about this business is so **life threatening** that I couldn't take an hour off to enjoy a lunch with Clients or friends without making several trips to the telephone. Or that I couldn't take a day off from the business without the whole world collapsing down around my ears.

APPLIED TO THE IMPORTANT "TIME IS MONEY"

For the first 14 years of my career I worked in a fit of frenzy. In those days I was busier doing 10 or 12 deals a year than I ever was when selling more than 200 homes annually in later years. When I slowed down and began applying time to what was important, rather than what was urgent, it became a source of negotiating power for me. Until that happened I was unable to appreciate the real meaning of the statement: **"Time is money"**. After that I also came to fully appreciate how true it is that in negotiating: **"The more time you take — the more money you make"**.

Time can be a source of negotiating power in many other ways. You can use time factors to create deadlines to get price reductions on your listings. You can use time factors can influence decisions of both Buyers and Sellers on offers and counter-offers. There's simply no end to the various ways we can use time as a source of power in the negotiating process.

KNOWLEDGE = NEGOTIATING POWER

Perhaps the most important source of negotiating power is "knowledge". The more you know about your product, the Seller, the Buyer, the other Salesperson and his company and so on, the more powerful you'll be in a negotiating session. It's important to take some time and get as much information as you possibly can about these matters before negotiations begin.

How many times have we heard someone say, "If I'd only known — about this or that — things would have been different", or how about these two; "If I'd only known, I'd have asked for more money", or "If I'd only known, I'd have waited a little longer". We've all made similar statements at some time in our lives. In most cases the information we lacked was readily available or easily accessible.

What we really meant when we made those statements was "If I'd only taken the time to find out in advance — things would have been a lot different". That's how powerful knowledge is in the negotiating process. It's powerful enough to make a huge difference.

For example, if you knew before presenting an offer, that a Seller desperately needed to sell, wouldn't that give you a powerful edge if you were representing the Buyer in a transaction? Or if you knew that your Sellers' home was the only one that was suitable to the Buyer making the offer, would that not give you a bundle of negotiating power if you were representing the Seller?

You can acquire additional knowledge during the actual negotiations that will put you in a more powerful position. When you're eyeball to eyeball with the other side, keep them talking until you get the information you want by applying the listening techniques we discussed in Chapter 1.

CHAPTER 8

BEWARE
INTIMIDATING TACTICS

Just as we employ various techniques to get information that gives us an edge, we have to be aware that experienced negotiators on the other side will use a variety of tactics to try and get information from us. Over the years I've had to contend with emotional outbursts, verbal bullying and sometimes even threats. The problem is we can never be sure if any type of emotional behavior is genuine or is simply a ploy to intimidate us.

DEALING WITH EMOTIONAL BEHAVIOR

The best way to handle these situations is to remain calm and relaxed. When the outburst is over, lower your voice to emphasize the difference between your mature behavior and their childish behavior.

Put the ball right back in their court by calmly asking for a specific explanation of what the fuss was all about. Then in a low voice, deal with the specific problem if there was one. If there wasn't, you know it was a ploy to rattle you that failed and continue to make your points.

We have to be aware that emotional outbursts are not always negotiating ploys. Sometimes when they occur during negotiations the reason is obvious. Other times it's not. Sometimes it's even expected. However its effect on negotiations is always negative if it isn't handled properly.

Experience has taught me that dealing with emotional behavior calmly and rationally, will usually nullify its negative effect, no matter what the reason for its onset. Handling emotional behavior calmly and rationally, in most situations, will turn the tables totally to your advantage.

THE
DOCTOR STORY

I remember an incident that occurred when presenting an offer on a listing of mine several years ago. This situation occurred before I learned the importance of presenting offers in my office rather than the Seller's home, as we discuss in Chapter 19.

Another Salesperson made arrangements to meet with my Sellers and me at their acreage to present an offer. Between the time I made the appointment and our arrival, my Seller who was a surgeon, had been called out on an emergency. We chatted with his wife while we waited for the good Doctor to return.

A MAJOR
NEGOTIATING BOO-BOO

When he finally arrived, he was really tired and irritable. The Salesman proceeded to present his offer. In an attempt to justify a lowball offer, he pulled out a list of a dozen things he said needed to be repaired before the Doctors' property would be worth what he was asking for it. In so doing, he committed a major negotiating boo-boo that Real Estate Salespeople and Brokers commit far too often when presenting offers. We deal with this in detail in Chapter 20.

The Doctor was so upset he got furious and threw the Salesman out of the house, insisting that he leave by the back door. At the same time the Doctor walked out the front door. He met the Salesman coming around the house and accompanied him down the long lane way to the road.

My driver was sitting in my limo on the road waiting for me. He overheard the Doctor giving the Salesman a tongue lashing for insulting him about the condition of his home and for inconsiderately parking his Mercedes in the gateway. Because of where the the Salesman parked his Mercedes, the Doctor couldn't get his own car from the roadway to the garage when he got home from the emergency.

When the Doctor returned I remained calm and relaxed. I suggested he should get a good night's sleep and we'd deal with the offer tomorrow. I told him I felt it was something we could work at improving and many times offers that start off like this work out great in the end. I made arrangements to meet him at his office the following day to work out a counter-offer.

In the meantime I discussed the situation with the other Salesperson. We agreed it was best he not be present at any future meetings with the Doctor.

PATIENCE
PREVAILED

The following day I met the Doctor at his office at the appointed time, and as has happened so often in my career, calmness and patience prevailed over anxiety and haste, and we were able to get a deal together.

Emotional outbursts, verbal bullying and threats should be avoided as negotiating tactics. They put the other side in a negative frame of mind and seldom, if ever, produce any positive results.

RECOGNIZE
THE SUCKER PUNCH

Another tactic that experienced negotiators might use when trying to get information that we may not want to disclose, is often referred to as the **Sucker Punch**. When used by a skillful negotiator the effect is similar to a boxer leaving an opening in his defense that is so inviting his opponent can't resist the temptation to throw a punch. When the opponent throws the punch however, without realizing it, he sets himself up for a devastating counter attack.

When experienced negotiators want to know something they feel they won't get from you by asking for the information directly, like the boxer setting his opponent up for the sucker punch, they'll use the indirect approach to get the information from you.

Sometimes they'll do this by making annoying statements or insinuations, to throw you off and get you talking. Other times they'll ask a cleverly worded question or series of questions, to try to accomplish the same thing.

WORST THING
SELLER CAN DO

Experience has convinced me that the absolute worst thing a Seller can do to themselves, is stay home while their home is being shown. Most Sellers have no idea how ill-equipped they are to handle the shrewd techniques employed by Buyers and other Salespeople who view their home. This is even more true today than it ever was before, with Buyer Agency becoming more and more prevalent all the time. I spend a considerable amount of time during each Listing Presentation convincing my Sellers they should leave every time their home is being shown.

A
PERFECT EXAMPLE

After showing a home one day, as we were leaving my Buyer said to the lady of the house, "I bet you'll be happy when this home sells. You'll be able to buy a home in your new city, get the family moved and get your life all back together again." She responded by saying, "Oh, we've already bought and we're moving on the weekend."

To the average person this seems like nothing more than an innocent bit of small talk. But what really happened here was, that without even realizing it, the Seller became a veritable information leak. What she really told my Buyer was that they were a lot more anxious to sell than they really should have let him know.

But it didn't end there. My Buyer followed up by saying, "Well that's the nice thing about being transferred by your company — they pay all the financing and moving costs for you. People like me couldn't afford to do what you guys did because I'd have to do it on my own."

I couldn't believe her response. She informed us that they didn't get any help from her husband's company, and that both she and her husband were unable to sleep at night, because they were worried about carrying two houses.

PLEASE
STEAL OUR HOME!

My Buyer made a lowball offer and stole himself a home. After it was all over he told me theirs was the only home he wanted. He would have paid full price if he had to. He also told me he would have offered considerably more to begin with, if the Seller hadn't been home and advised him to steal the place.

I tell that story during every Listing Presentation I make, to illustrate why my Sellers should leave their home every time it gets shown. It's a perfect example of how to use the **Sucker Punch** as a negotiating technique. That's why most of my Clients trip over each other trying to get out of their home every time it gets shown.

HOW TO AVOID
THE SUCKER PUNCH

If you're dealing with a smooth, experienced negotiator on the other side, it may take a while for you to realize that you've become a genuine information leak, or as the British say, "You've been had". Here are some steps you can take to avoid being the victim of the sucker punch in any situation:

1) Take your time before answering questions posed by the other side. Try to analyze why the question is being asked before answering it.

2) Be aware that irritating statements are often employed to get you to say things you wouldn't normally say. The best approach is to ignore them as though they were never said. If you remain calm and ignore the use

of irritating statements by the other side to get you riled, the tactic will be dropped because it's not being effective.

3) Make light of questions or comments you feel are being used to draw you in, by simply identifying them as guesses by the other side or suggesting they're irrelevant to the negotiations at hand.

HIGHLY
EFFECTIVE TACTIC

The **Sucker Punch** is an excellent technique. It can be used effectively by either side in a negotiating session to uncover valuable information. When combined with good listening skills, it's a highly effective tactic that every negotiator should learn to use with as much skill and competence as possible.

CHAPTER 9

NEGOTIATING IS
LIKE PLAYING GOLF

I've always said that various aspects of professional

selling were analogous to different aspects of playing golf.

During my Mini-Rallies® I frequently draw a parallel, demonstrating how those who remain in the top one or two percent of any field of sales, are similar to those professional golfers who continually survive the cut, and play in every major golf tournament.

In my earlier book, *Championship Selling*, I stated that using my "Championship Selling System" to sell real estate was a Real Estate Agent's ticket to play in the championship round. Oddly enough, negotiating is more than a little bit like playing golf as well.

PRACTICE
MAKES PERFECT

You might be a good golfer but you won't remain good if you don't practice. The same thing applies to negotiating. If we're negotiating all the time we can remain quite good.

However just like it is with golf, if we want to improve our game, a few practice rounds where we concentrate on improving our weaknesses will make us even better. So hold some practice sessions with your colleagues or spouse, or anyone else who's willing to help. You be yourself and let them be the other side.

MOCK
NEGOTIATING SESSIONS

I'm talking here about role playing — conducting

mock negotiating sessions. Professional negotiators use these sessions to help prepare for major events they'll be participating in. During mock negotiating sessions you can experiment with various tactics and approaches. This enables you to test their effectiveness without suffering any negative consequences if they don't work. It's far better to know in advance that certain arguments or answers are inadequate than to suffer embarrassment during an actual negotiating session.

ROLE PLAY
WITH SELLERS

As a result of the variety of Agency relationships becoming prevalent in the industry, more and more of the Top Real Estate Salespeople are conducting role playing sessions with their Sellers.

This is a great way to ensure that things go smoothly at Offer Presentation time. A little coaching as to how the Seller should act in response to certain types of offers, questions, comments, behaviors, tactics, and so on, can have a major impact on the outcome of the negotiating process.

A PROVEN
CONCEPT

The value of role playing is well known in the negotiating field. It's a proven concept. Master negotiators will tell you that conducting a mock negotiating session as part of their preparation for the real thing, often determines whether the outcome of a negotiating session will be a success or a failure.

It's a great way to learn how to ask the right questions; to practice being a nice guy; to learn the art of being patient; to practice being calm; and to hone your listening skills.

Role playing is commonly used in sports — especially in football; it's used by many sales organizations and it's used extensively by lawyers to sharpen their skills at cross-examining witnesses, addressing the court and addressing the juries. And it's a particularly effective method of practicing and sharpening your negotiating skills.

SECTION TWO

NEGOTIATING WITH SELLERS

CHAPTER 10

KNOCK, KNOCK, KNOCKIN' ON THE SELLERS' DOOR

When doing Listing Presentations we're really into

serious negotiations about all kinds of issues. In the next several Chapters we're going to deal with negotiating strategies concerning Sellers; strategies that have helped me win nearly every listing competition I've been involved in over the years; strategies that have enabled me to carry an inventory of more than 50 active listings at all times, for a long number of years during my real estate career.

We're going to be dealing primarily with how we handle things after we arrive at the Seller's home to make our Listing Presentation. However, before we knock on the Seller's door to keep our appointment, I want to touch briefly on a few items leading up to that point. I also want to touch on a few items which are important, that have to do with listings in general.

WHO DO WE
NEGOTIATE WITH?

When it's established that I'll be doing a Listing Presentation, I get all the information needed to prepare a Market Analysis. Before I set the appointment we have a discussion about who actually owns the property. I want to know if they have a partner or husband or wife who owns the property with them. In other words I want to know who I really have to negotiate with in the final analysis. Even though I always pull title on the property by FAX this doesn't necessarily show the true owners of the property.

If there are two people involved, and in most cases there seems to be, I explain it's imperative that we all meet together. I point out that it'll take between an hour and a half and two hours for me to cover everything with them. I want them both to hear my full Presentation and feel comfortable with me. Experience has taught me, there is little point going on a Presentation if both parties to decisions concerning the property are not there.

First of all, you have a far better chance of listing the property if all parties to the decision making process are present. Secondly, your relationship with the Sellers will be much better because their expectations and understanding of your role will be the same. And thirdly, we have to remember that in all these situations, aside from all the other issues we're negotiating, **we're also negotiating the use of the most precious commodity we have — our time.**

PREPARE PROPERLY
BUT KEEP IT SIMPLE

We've already discussed the fact that one of the keys for any negotiation to succeed, is proper preparation. So after we set the appointment we have to prepare the material for our Presentation. But I believe the most important thing concerning preparation is to keep it simple.

I had that point driven home rather dramatically a number of years ago. A prominent lawyer who lived in a somewhat exclusive area called me to do a Market Analysis for him. Back then we didn't have computers. As a result, we didn't have such things as legal descriptions, tax information and other data at our finger tips like we do now.

In any case, he did the smart thing and decided to give me the listing. I began asking the usual questions like, "What's your legal description? What's the lot size? How much are your taxes?" and so on. Finally he said, "Oh, what the heck", and went over to his china cabinet. He pulled out this beautiful Presentation that one of my competitors had spent at least a day preparing.

It was an expensive booklet with colored photos of his property, colored photos of her company's head office, a statement outlining their marketing plan, all kinds of maps and a detailed history of the area. But more important than all that, it had the answers to all my questions.

When he handed it to me I said, "Boy you must have been impressed!" I've never forgotten his answer. He said, "No, far from it. My wife and I were confused by all that. But now we're impressed. You impress us! And we feel you can get our home sold. All the fancy paperwork in the world will never do that."

INFORMATION OVERLOAD

After that experience I quit using fancy Listing Presentations. If they were confusing to a highly intelligent, well educated person like my Seller was, they surely represented information overload to the average Seller. In addition, they provide Sellers with the best excuse in the world for not listing with you, at the time you make your Presentation. I.E. "Let me study your booklet and I'll get back to you after I digest what's in it."

I don't know of a single situation where I've lost a listing because someone did a fancier Presentation than I did. But I could give you numerous examples like the one I just mentioned.

THE PSYCHOLOGY
OF SOLD

I use a simple Presentation folder with the word "SOLD" in large green letters across the front. The reason the world "Sold" is in green letters, rather than the customary red letters used on most real estate signs, is that the purpose of having the world "SOLD" printed on the folders is for psychological impact.

A number of studies indicate that for obvious reasons when many people see the colour red, they subconsciously think it means stop or danger, and it often brings back unpleasant memories. For this same reason it's not advisable to use a red pen or pencil during negotiations either.

In fact some psychologists suggest that not only should you avoid the use of red pens, pencils and printed material whenever you want to make the greatest psychological impact during negotiations, but you should also avoid wearing red clothing. Blues, greens and tans are recommended. Apparently these are far more relaxing to both sides.

I'VE COME
TO SELL IT

When I do a Listing Presentation, or present an offer, I always lay my Presentation folder on the table in full view of everyone present. While we're doing our small talk the world "SOLD" is constantly staring everyone in the face.

When I open the folder the first thing that falls out on the table are two bright green "SOLD" stickers and two "Conditionally Sold" stickers. The psychological effect of having all these "Solds" floating around is unbelievable. It conveys a message that I've come to sell their property — not just to list it!

I've had numerous cases, where the lady of the house would pick the "Sold" stickers up, place them on the refrigerator with another Agent's fridge magnet and say, "Marilyn, I'm going to leave these right here until you sell it". When this happens I know I've got a listing before I even start my Presentation.

FORCE SELLER
TO CONFRONT REALITY

When negotiating with Sellers I've discovered that a key to writing listings at the proper price is to have the Seller conduct his own Market Analysis. This has become a crucial step in my Listing Presentation. It forces the Seller to confront reality and we'll discuss the exact procedure I use to accomplish this in more detail in Chapter 12.

In addition to putting the usual items for a Listing Presentation in my Presentation folder, my assistant encloses all the relevant computer work. This includes enough extra computer printouts of each of the sold, active and expired listings for me to provide a copy of each to the Sellers so they can analyze the data themselves, and confirm for me what their home should be listed at.

On my way to the appointment I have my driver take me by a few of the comparables. I analyze the data and determine what I feel the subject is worth. But I never write the value on anything. I always leave that open for final determination by the Sellers, after they do a thorough analysis of the computer data themselves, during my Presentation.

TAKE CONTROL IMMEDIATELY

When I arrive at the home, I introduce myself and take control immediately. As I head for the dining room table I say, "I'll put my books here on the table because we're going to need a fair bit of room to work, and spread things out so you can see everything I've brought with me".

AN ESSENTIAL WIN-WIN REQUIREMENT

Immediately after I put my books on the table I say, "Now, would one of you be kind enough to take me on a tour of your home?" If they say, "Oh you go through houses all the time, just take a run through on your own," I reply, "No, I'm really not comfortable doing that. It's your home. You know it best. Come and give me the grand tour." After an exchange like that one of them will always take you on the tour.

The reason for insisting on them accompanying you on the tour is this. One of the most essential requirements for Win-Win negotiations to succeed is to develop an atmosphere of mutual trust. This is an opportunity for positive interaction between you and the Seller. It's an opportunity to learn about the Sellers' goals. It allows you to get to know each other a bit before you sit down to do business. Just like the Seller wants to learn about you, you want to learn as much as you can about these people before you do your Presentation.

Don't get your note pad out and write things down. Instead, pay total attention to them and what they are saying. Ask nice questions that will keep them talking about themselves. Remember the more you get people to talk about themselves the better they like you. The more they talk the greater the volume of useful information they'll provide.

You can talk to them about why they're selling. If they're moving to another city tell them you'll have a top Real Estate Agent from that city get in touch with them. Then you can earn a referral fee if that Agent sells them a home. Or if they're being transferred, they might know others from their Company who are being transferred and could also use your services.

DECISION
MAKERS TOUR

It's rare that both parties go with you on the tour. But here's the interesting thing. It's usually the **decision maker** who accompanies you through the home. And you often learn some amazing things as you go, that they didn't tell you on the phone when you made the appointment.

I've had Sellers tell me things such as, "If the atmosphere seems a little on the cold side here tonight it's because we're getting divorced." Or, "If my husband doesn't seem that interested, it's because this is a second marriage for both of us. It's my home and the final decision is really up to me, but I do rely on him for some advice."

Having the Seller take you on a tour of the home is one of the most productive negotiating techniques you'll ever employ. It allows you to have positive interaction with the Seller and develop an atmosphere of trust before you make your Presentation.

If you use this technique correctly, you'll get all kinds of information you won't get on the telephone, or by sitting down at the table with both parties. And you'll nearly always find out which of the Sellers is the **decision maker**. This gives you some valuable insight into how you have to treat their mate or partner.

CHAPTER 11

FORGET
THE TWO-STEP

Should I use a one-step approach or a two-step

approach when I go to do a Market Analysis. That's a question I get asked at nearly every Mini-Rally® I do. And it's a question that's asked by seasoned veterans as well as Salespeople who are new to the real estate business.

MASTER THE
ONE-STEP

Some Real Estate Agents inspect the property and come back later with an opinion of value. They attempt to list the property at that time. I absolutely love it when I go up against someone using this approach. Except in unusual circumstances where the other Agent is the Seller's mother, or something like that, I know I'm going to win for sure. There simply isn't any question about it.

I can make any Salesperson using the two-step approach look like a rank amateur. All I have to do is show the Seller how to evaluate his own property by following the procedure outlined in Chapter 12, using data that is readily available to everyone in the business, including the Salesperson who hasn't gotten back to the Seller yet. As a result I win virtually every competition for a listing where I'm competing with someone using the two-step approach.

From a negotiating perspective there are all kinds of reasons why one should master the one-step approach, go in with a positive attitude, do a combination Market Analysis and Listing Presentation and leave with a listing.

The one-step approach demonstrates far more confidence in your ability. In addition, it makes eminent good sense from a time management point of view. And I know from experience that those who use the one-step approach enjoy a much higher closing ratio on listing appointments. It simply makes good negotiating sense to master using the one-step approach.

UNIQUE PROPERTIES

We've all encountered properties that are so unique, evaluating them presents an impossible challenge to even the most experienced Salespeople. Even in cases like this I still write the listing when I'm there. I leave the price and date blank and on completion of a professional appraisal the Seller and I determine the listing price by phone. At that time I simply insert the price in the listing, have a copy delivered to the Seller and proceed then to have the listing processed.

In this case, the listing is not legally valid at the time it is signed. However it makes good sense to get the Seller to sign the listing agreement when you're there anyway, because he'll feel morally obligated to you when he signs it. In effect you eliminate the competition, because it's unlikely he'll deal with anyone else concerning the listing after he signs your agreement.

CHAPTER 12

PRICING
THE LISTING

After touring the home, I go back to the dining room

table and take control of the seating arrangements. I get both parties to sit across the table from me so I can see their reactions and look them in the eye.

After we get everybody situated at the table the very first thing we deal with is the value of their home. When you present an offer, if the first thing you deal with is the price being offered, the balance of the negotiations will proceed in a much more relaxed and friendly manner. The same thing applies to a Listing Presentation. If you deal with the value of the property at the outset, the balance of the Listing Presentation will be a lot more comfortable and easy for everyone.

There's nothing more stressful for everyone concerned, than when a Salesperson presenting an offer reads through the thing clause by clause; tells the Seller the appliances are included; discusses the possession date at length; and finally gets to the price a half hour later. All the Seller wanted to know from the beginning was the big secret — how much? So when you do a Listing Presentation, get the "How Much" question out of the way at the outset.

WHY I KNOW
WHAT IT'S WORTH

I hand them both a copy of the computer print-outs of the sold listings, the current listings and the expired listings in their area. Then I say to them, "Now, I know how much your home is worth. But before I tell you what it's worth, I want you to go through these sheets with me, so you can see — why I know — what it's worth."

Notice I said, "Why I know what it's worth", and not, "How I arrived at the price". Saying "Why I know what your home is worth", demonstrates confidence. It gets the message across that I know what it's worth; that I'm not trying to figure out what it's worth — I know!

People love looking at these computer print-outs. It relaxes them. It puts them at ease, much like looking at a map does during a Buyer Interview. In fact, the computer print-outs actually serve as a bonding agent between a Real Estate Salesperson and his Clients during Listing Presentations. Maps do the same thing during Buyer Interviews.

CONFRONTING
REALITY

I act as the chairman of the meeting and together we get down to work. I give them each a highlighter and explain the abbreviations for such things as fireplaces and so on. We go through the list of solds first. Prior to arriving I always place a small mark on my copies beside the ones that are good comparables.

We talk about the first comparable; agree that it's a valid one and make adjustments for the differences. Then they highlight it on their copy and I highlight it on mine. When we're finished with the first comparable we proceed to the second one. We discuss it; agree it's a good comparable and once again make adjustments for the differences. Again they highlight it on their copies and I highlight it on mine. Then we proceed to the third comparable and the fourth and fifth and sixth and so on, until we get to the end of the list of solds.

Often they'll recognize a property that sold, and are a little surprised to learn it sold for a whole lot less than the neighbor had told them he sold it for. Other times they'll know a property that I haven't been through, and their input can help determine if it's a good comparable or not. Before long they begin to feel just like a Real Estate Agent trying to place a value on a property.

OUR HOME
IS WORTH ABOUT X$

Usually when you get to the bottom of the list of Sold properties, if you've done a good job of chairing the session they'll say something like, "Well it looks like our home is worth about $150,000." They may not like it. They may have thought it was worth $20,000 more. But like I stated earlier, this process of making them analyze the data themselves forces them to confront reality.

At this point I'll say, "I'm going to make Salespeople out of you guys yet if I'm not careful, but don't set the price just yet. We should look at the active listings first to see what our competition is, and at the recent expired listings to see why they didn't sell. That will verify what the listing price should be."

Then we go through the actives the same way we did the solds. After we've discussed each comparable, they highlight it on their copies of the printouts and I highlight it on mine. While going through these I emphasize the length of time they've been on the market and also the listing price. They see then, that generally speaking the higher the price, the longer the property sits on the market.

Then we go through the expired listings in the same manner. They usually conclude these didn't sell because they were priced too high, and/or, were in poorer condition than the competition was.

As we are analyzing the computer sheets I emphasize that what we're looking at here, are records of actual sales; listings that are currently active and haven't sold yet; and listings that have expired and didn't sell because the Sellers had expectations that were unrealistic in today's market.

At the end of this exercise they tell me what their home is worth. Sometimes it will be lower than my estimate, and sometimes it'll be higher. But it's nearly always within $3,000 to $5,000 of my original estimate.

MOTIVATION
AND TIME CONSTRAINTS

Now it's a matter of determining the final listing price. A key to doing this is to determine how strong their motivation to sell is. Usually, though not always, the motivation will hinge on a time factor. How much time do they have to sell their home?

In the case of out-of-town transfers, there's usually a shorter time frame. If they're transferring without a company guarantee the time element is even more critical. Time is often a factor even in local moves. Being in a new home before the school year begins is often a key factor.

Sometimes they've signed a contract to build a new home and have to get the present one sold. Perhaps the deal hinges on a favorable interest rate which is only available for a specified time. In other cases there are financial and personal problems. In these situations too, the time factor is often more important.

As discussed in Chapter 7, both time and knowledge give us power when we're negotiating. Knowing their time constraints will give you a tremendous amount of power in the pricing process during the Listing Presentation. The same is true when it comes to negotiating price reductions and offers later on. Have a good frank discussion with them about the time frame in which they have to sell the home.

FINE-TUNING
THE PRICE

It's not unusual in many areas for it to take about 90 days to sell certain properly priced homes, depending on condition, price range, type of home and location. The more expensive the home, the longer it takes. So I point out that if they want the home to sell quickly we have to fine-tune the listing price accordingly.

This is where the computer is the best tool you ever laid hands on. I point out how all Buyers give the Salesperson they're dealing with a price range they want to buy in and these price ranges tend to be in increments of $10,000. If we conclude the value of their home was at the most $145,000, I'll show them the computer print outs where prices start at $135,000. I show them the section that includes everything between $135,000 and $145,000.

I point out that when Salespeople are making appointments to show properties in a certain price range they do two things. First of all, they only show from three to five properties to a Buyer at a time. Secondly, they start at the beginning of the price range and make appointments on the first three to five that appear suitable.

I point out that Salespeople often sell their Buyers the first day out. If they don't, they simply make more appointments by moving up a little higher in the price range. If the Sellers want or need a quick sale, then it's extremely important their property be positioned as close as possible to the beginning of the price range in which they fall.

So my question to them is this, "Where do they want to be positioned in order to get more Salespeople working on selling their property, so it'll sell in their time frame?"

WE PAID MORE
SO WE CAN'T SELL YET

It's usually easier to get Sellers to price their home right if their motivation involves a time factor. However the time factor isn't a concern with all Sellers. Sometimes they'll say, "We can't sell yet. We paid more for this place than we can get for it right now." In that case I ask them if they sold now, would they be buying again locally.

If the answer is yes, I point out that it's as broad as it is long. Why not buy something they like better now, and wait for it to go up in value, instead of sitting in their present home which they don't like and waiting for it to go up. In most cases they simply haven't thought the situation through. After I explain it to them in this way they'll often go ahead and list with me, and buy something they like better right away.

NO LISTING —
NO REDUCTION

In some cases the Seller wants to try the listing at a higher price no matter what statistics say, even if there is a need to sell quickly. In that case I still take the listing. But I try to establish a program of regular price reductions, where every two or three weeks we reduce the price if we're not getting action, until it's priced properly.

If you don't have the listing you won't be the one who gets the reduction. Whoever has the listing will get it. **There's only one way to get yourself in a position to negotiate a reduction to any listing, overpriced or otherwise, and that is to write the listing in the first place.** Always remember, that he who has the listings gets the price reductions — and the commissions that follow. It's really that simple!

NO SUCH THING
AS A BAD LISTING

As Salespeople we also encounter the Seller who has very little motivation to sell, who insists that his property be listed outrageously high, knowing full well that his price is totally unreasonable, yet is prepared to wait forever so it seems, to get his price. Even in that case I still take the listing. As far as I'm concerned there is no such thing as a bad listing.

On the other hand I'm the first to agree that there is such a thing as a "Bad Seller". These guys fall into several categories and we simply don't need any of them in our lives — whether their listing is over-priced or even if it's priced right on the money.

First of all, there's the unreasonable type who in spite of all the evidence to the contrary doesn't believe any of it. Not only does he want you to list his property outrageously high, but he actually expects you to spend all your time and money trying to perform an impossible miracle for him.

There's also the type who considers hiring a Real Estate Agent tantamount to leasing his own slave. When he gives you his listing, as far as he's concerned he's got the God-given right to literally run your life, until the day the listing sells or expires.

Then there's the type who expects you to work flat out at getting his home sold and only wants to pay you a fraction of what you're worth for doing so. For some strange reason he thinks you should pay him to be your Seller.

Unfortunately there always seems to be Salespeople willing to accommodate these types of Sellers. The fact is dealing with any of them is simply not worth the grief and aggravation they cause you.

NOT A
WASTE OF TIME

I've heard Salespeople say they wouldn't waste their time writing an overpriced listing, under any circumstances. I disagree with that position wholeheartedly. Provided the Seller is fully aware that his listing is overpriced, and provided he doesn't expect you to spend your time and money to work miracles for him, having such a listing is certainly not a waste of time. I've taken numerous listings of this kind over the years, and in every case they've made me nothing but money.

The key here is the type of Seller. If he falls into the "Bad Seller" category we discussed earlier, having such a listing is definitely a waste of time. In fact I won't even write a well-priced listing for a Seller who falls into the "Bad Seller" category, because even in that case it's a waste of time. The grief and aggravation this kind of Seller brings into your life is simply not worth the effort required to deal with it.

THE VALUE OF
OVER-PRICED LISTINGS

Some overpriced listings sell. Others end up being priced right in the future, when a Seller's circumstances change and he becomes more serious. But that's all beside the point.

Some of the best Clients and Customers I've ever had came as a result of having over-priced listings. One over-priced listing I carried for several years illustrates their value better than anything else I can think of.

My Seller knew from the beginning that his property was drastically over-priced. He wasn't motivated at all. But as he said at the time, "Marilyn, if I don't have a ticket I can't win. I know I'm probably being foolish, but maybe some fool will fall into town and pay me my price." As he put it, he was motivated by "luck"!

So I gave him his ticket. I listed his home, put it in the MLS catalogue for him and put my sign on his lawn. That's all I was willing to give him at the price he was asking, and he was more than happy with that arrangement.

He was the publisher of one of the local newspapers and he knew all kinds of people. For two years he thought about me as his Real Estate Agent because every morning when he went to work and every evening when he came home he saw my name flapping in the breeze on the sign on his lawn. My sign made me a part of his life every day. He sent me all kinds of business.

HIS
CIRCUMSTANCES CHANGED

What happens with most over-priced listings happened with him two years later. His circumstances changed. He got transferred to Toronto and at that time we priced it right and I sold it quickly to a Doctor. Subsequently, both the son and daughter of the Buyer bought homes from me and so did some of their friends.

Since then the Buyer himself has bought a couple of income properties from me. Both the Seller and the Buyer still send me the odd Client. During the overpriced period I had several sign calls who came for Buyer Interviews and bought properties from me.

But the important point is this. When I look back on the computer, that over-priced listing earned me in excess of $150,000 in commissions. And it's still earning me money today through referrals and repeat business I receive from those Clients who came to me as a result of having the listing in the first place. This is but one of numerous examples I could tell you about.

LEARN TO
USE THEM WISELY

Over-priced listings are not a waste of time and can earn big money for Real Estate Agents who learn to use them wisely. The next time you hear someone say they didn't write a listing because it was over-priced, ask them what the Seller's name, address and phone number is. Then go check it out.

Remember there's no such thing as a bad listing, but there is such a thing as a bad Seller. If the owners fall into the "Bad Seller" category that we discussed earlier don't take the listing. If they fall into the "Good Seller" category write the listing up for a long term. Give the Seller a cancellation agreement like we discuss in Chapter 14, so you don't have to keep relisting the property. Put your sign on the lawn and the odds are it'll make you nothing but money.

CHAPTER 13

NEGOTIATING HIGHER
LISTING COMMISSIONS

There's a disturbing trend out there that sees more

and more Real Estate Agents falling into a rut that they often never get out of. And a rut by the way is nothing more than an open ended grave.

PRESCRIPTION FOR FINANCIAL SUICIDE

A Seller decides to interview several Agents and reverse negotiations begin. "I'll list it for 4%," says the first. "Give it to me and I'll only charge you 3%," says the second. "I'll only charge you 2% if I sell it myself," says the third.

The fourth says, "These guys are all ripping you off, I'll only charge you 2% if I sell it myself and I'll kick you back 50% of my commission if you repurchase through me." There are Salespeople out there who are literally paying both Sellers and Buyers to let them be their Agent. It's nothing but a prescription for financial suicide.

As Real Estate Professionals we're supposed to be in business. One of the main purposes of being in business is to generate a profit, so that ourselves and our families can enjoy a higher standard of living. We can't do that if we work for nothing.

REASON FOR HIGH INDUSTRY TURNOVER

The real estate business suffers an unforgivable, embarrassing and unnecessary turnover of Salespeople. I believe one of the main reasons for this situation is, that as an industry, we do a very poor job of teaching Salespeople to become good negotiators.

In many of the jurisdictions where this book will be read, the industry is prohibited by law from fixing in any way, the rate of commission its members are allowed to charge. That doesn't mean we're prohibited from teaching Brokers and Salespeople how to become better negotiators, or teaching them that they have to charge enough for their services so they can earn a decent living and stay off the welfare rolls. This can be done without conspiring to fix commissions. To think otherwise is ridiculous, to say the least.

Apparently governments have the right to use our tax dollars to promote to the public, the dubious benefits of Real Estate Agents using the cut-rate commission concept, working for nothing and going broke. Surely then, we have the right to use a little of what they don't tax away from us, to extol the virtues of Real Estate Salespeople and Brokers charging enough commission so they can pay their bills, avoid bankruptcy and stay in business for a while.

Since the commission issue is so vital to our well-being as Real Estate Agents, I'm going to discuss the approach I use to make sure I get properly paid on every listing I write.

OPPORTUNITY FOR HIGHER COMMISSION

When I'm doing a listing I fill in the commission automatically at the rate charged by the vast majority of local

Agents, which is 7%. Sometimes the Sellers query the amount or suggest they understand commissions are negotiable. When they do I absolutely love it. It gives me an opportunity to get an even higher commission. That may not have been what they had in mind when they brought the subject up, but the fact is it presents a fantastic opportunity for me to sell them on the merits of using higher commissions and bonuses as the tremendously powerful marketing tools they are.

Even if they don't bring it up I always do, because I feel I have an obligation to do so. In my opinion I'd be rendering them a grave injustice if I didn't point out all the tremendous benefits a Seller receives by listing at a higher commission rather than a lower one.

A BARE
MINIMUM

First of all I acknowledge that commissions are negotiable. Then I point out that I charge 7% as a "Bare Minimum" because of the quality of service I provide and the results that I get.

On top of that, I've been in the business over 30 years and as a matter of policy, I've never varied the minimum percentage I charge between one customer and another.

I point out he's talking about my paycheck. My paycheck is like his. I count on it like he does. I ask him how he'd feel if he went to work tomorrow, and his boss asked him to take a cut in pay and still work as hard as he does now? Yet that's exactly what he's asking me to do — take a cut in pay and work flat out at getting his home sold.

BENEFITS OF
HIGHER COMMISSION

I suggest that what we should be discussing are the benefits of paying a higher commission rather than a lower one. In all my years in the business I've never experienced a situation where a property sold faster because it was listed at a lower commission. However I can tell them story after story about properties selling quicker because they were listed at a higher than average commission, or had some type of bonus on them to excite the Real Estate Agents.

I ask him when he goes to work tomorrow, would he get **excited** and work harder the rest of the week, if the boss told him he'd receive a 15% bonus for doing so. When he answers "Yes", I say "O.K. now, why not give me some ammunition to get all the Agents out there **excited** so they work harder at selling your home. Why don't we list it at 8%, instead of 7% like most properties in this area are listed at?"

I open the MLS catalogue and show him that the commission split on nearly every property is based as though 7% is being split 50/50 between the listing and selling offices. I explain that in some cases the Listing Agent may have the property listed at a lower commission, and is offering a higher split to the selling Agent, but in our case it doesn't matter because I don't follow that practice in any event.

REAL ESTATE AGENTS
ARE NORMAL PEOPLE

I point out that Real Estate Agents tend to be fairly

normal people. When making appointments to show property they tend to pay close attention to the commission they'll receive if they sell it. In my own case I simply avoid showing properties with lower commissions altogether. Why would I show a property with a lower commission when I can show my Buyers any number of others on which I'll earn a bigger paycheck.

BUSINESS CARD POKER

To demonstrate this point even more dramatically I often play a little game with the Seller. I call it business card poker. I lay three business cards on the table blank side up. I say to my Seller, "Let's settle this commission question by changing roles here for a minute. You be the Real Estate Agent and I'll be the Buyer. I've just come into your office to buy a home. You've got three homes that would suit me perfectly. They're all identical in every way, just like these three business cards.

This first one is listed at 3% which is less than half what you're used to getting. This other one is listed at 7% which is the minimum you're used to getting. This last one is listed at 8%. In fact if you sell it, on a $100,000 home you'll make yourself a nice little bonus of $1000. Now which of these three homes are you going to be inclined to sell me?" He knows the answer. End of story.

I'LL BE NEGOTIATING ON THEIR BEHALF

I also discuss the fact they're hiring me to represent them in their dealings, not just with other Real Estate

Agents but also with the public. This means that I'll be negotiating with others on their behalf. The type of offer they receive on their property will depend to a great degree on the type of negotiator I happen to be.

OTHER AGENTS
AND FIRST TIME BUYERS

So I ask him, "If I was the kind of Agent who gave away my commission easily, are you going to feel comfortable having me represent you? If I handle my own money that way, what do you think I'm apt to do with yours?"

"When another Agent calls wanting to know how much your home will sell for, what do you think my answer will be if I'm not even capable of negotiating a commission that reflects what I'm really worth?" Am I going to be the kind of Salesperson who'll say, "Oh, let's try about $20,000 less" or am I going to be a strong negotiator on your behalf and say, "We listed that home for the right price and we think we should get what we're asking for it".

"What do you think will happen with a young couple buying their first home, who falls in love with your home and then get a little bit nervous about what they're doing. If I caved in and gave away my commission just like that, do you think I'll be strong enough to see them through to a deal, or will I wimp out with them, and blow what should be a sure sale for you?"

"So tell me honestly, do you think I'll be capable of negotiating with another Salesperson or a prospective Buyer and getting you the best offer possible on your property, if I was willing to give away my paycheck before we even get started?"

NOBODY WANTS
TO LIST FOR LESS

When you deal with the commission issue in this manner you're selling a higher commission as a marketing tool. After using any of these approaches it's not unusual to have Sellers list at a higher commission right on the spot. In other cases they'll call back later and increase the commission, when they become a little more anxious. No one ever wants to list for less than my minimum rate.

ANOTHER POWERFUL
MARKETING TOOL

In addition to a higher commission I explain that another powerful marketing tool is a bonus of $1000 or $2000 to the selling Salesperson. If they don't want to consider it now, this is something they can consider later if we don't get sufficient action.

MY
TEXAS STORY

In this regard I often think of a Seller of mine who was transferred to Texas a few years ago. Three times we thought we were getting an offer, and three times we ended up being the bridesmaid instead of the bride.

My Seller called and said, "You know Marilyn I've been thinking about that bonus idea you talked about when you listed this place. I think at least one of those Agents might have pushed a little harder if I'd listened to you, and my house would probably be sold now.

However I didn't listen to you and that's my fault. Forget the $1000 bonus we talked about then, and let's put a $2000 bonus on for the selling Agent right now."

Before the amendment adding the bonus was processed through the board, another Saleslady showed the home. She told me her Buyers were trying to decide between our listing and another. She thought they were really leaning towards the other home. It looked like we were going to be the bridesmaid again.

I told her we'd just put a bonus of $2000 on our listing for the selling Agent. I suggested she now had a bit of incentive to alter the direction her people were leaning in. Within an hour we had an acceptable offer and sold the home to her happy Buyers. You've never seen anyone so eager to pay a bonus in your life as my Seller was that night.

I tell that story to the Sellers on every Listing Presentation I do, to demonstrate how paying a bonus will work to their advantage. **It's a powerful marketing tool!**

QUICKER SALE
AND HIGHER PRICE

Usually when you put a bonus or higher commission on a listing it doesn't cost the Seller anything. There's only a certain group of Salespeople who ever work on a given listing. When you put on a bonus or higher commission you get a larger group interested in working on selling the property. Because of that you'll often get a better price which means more money to the Seller.

In addition to getting a better price, the property often sells faster because of the higher commission or bonus. This usually means more money in the Sellers' pocket as well, especially if he's moving and has already bought another home. So does a higher commission or bonus really cost the Seller anything? In most cases — the answer is no!

MUSIC
TO MY EARS

Don't be afraid to earn yourself a reputation among your peers in the business, as well as the public, for never cutting commission and for putting your listings on the market with higher commissions and bonuses. I enjoyed that reputation for years.

When I talk about using higher commission and bonuses as marketing tools to help sell your listings, I'm not talking about inflating the price to do so. There isn't a marketing tool on the face of the earth that will cause any property that is drastically overpriced to sell. Inflating the price simply defeats the purpose of putting on a higher commission or bonus. In fact it defeats the purpose of using any other marketing tools as well.

Time after time when I'd be writing listings, Sellers who were referred to me by one of my Clients would say, "We know you never cut your commission and we really understand why. We also know that the bonus idea really helped sell our friends' home, so we'll look at doing that in a month if nothing is happening by then." Believe me, nothing comes close to sounding as good as that does. It's music to my ears.

SEIZE
THE OPPORTUNITY

Salespeople from all companies paid close attention to my listings because they always got at least the minimum they expected, and often a bigger paycheck, when they sold one of my listings. My listings sold because of it!

In this business, opportunity comes knocking regularly. But for some reason many Salespeople don't recognize it even when it comes begging. So the next time a Seller suggests that he thought commissions were negotiable, seize the golden opportunity you've been given, to negotiate a higher commission for yourself. Sell your Client on all the benefits a Seller receives as a result of listing at a higher commission or with a bonus for the selling Agent, or both.

When it comes to negotiating fees and commissions, one of the hardest lessons we have to learn as Real Estate Salespeople is, that a lower price for our services is seldom synonymous with greater value for our clients.

CHAPTER 14

LIST FOR MINIMUM 6 MONTHS TO 1 YEAR

I write all my listings for a minimum of six months. If

the property is below average, or for some reason is likely to take longer to sell, I take the listing for a longer term. Certain types of properties I take for a minimum of a year.

NOBODY WINS WHEN
SELLER FRUSTRATED

Several years ago I adopted a policy where I give any Seller an "unconditional release" from their listing if they're unhappy with my services, or if for any reason whatsoever they want to get out of the listing.

It was evident to me that Real Estate Agents are the biggest losers when they force an unhappy Seller to continue to deal with them, by giving them a "conditional release" from their listing. Nobody wins when an unhappy Seller is frustrated by having to wait until a listing expires before he can deal with someone else.

Study upon study has proven that businesses which place a higher emphasis on customer satisfaction, are far more successful than those who do not. In fact one study indicates that by forcing an incompatible relationship on a customer, over a period of a lifetime through the ripple effect he has on others, can cause up to 140 additional people to not deal with you.

THE CUSTOMER
IS ALWAYS RIGHT

I recently read a book about Sam Walton, who was the founder of Walmart stores and one of the richest men in America. Walmart is probably the most successful retail organization the world has ever seen.

Walmart employs over 600,000 people. There are two rules that every Walmart employee is expected to live by. The first is: "The customer is **always** right." Not sometimes, not most of the time — but **always!** The second rule is : "If in doubt refer back to rule #1." In my opinion, too many business people including Real Estate Agents, make the fatal mistake of ignoring rule #2 far too often.

So I tell every Seller who lists with me, that if at any time they're unhappy with my services, or if for any other reason whatsoever they want to cancel their listing, I'll give them the cancellation "unconditionally". All they have to do is ask. It's that simple.

SELLERS
COULD CARE LESS

I offer to give them a letter to this effect signed by myself and my Broker. About 99% of the time they say, "Don't worry about the letter, Marilyn. I can tell you're sincere. Your word is good enough for me."

After I explain my policy to them, my Sellers could care less if I put a ten year term on their listing. I point out that by putting a longer term on the listing it saves both of us, the time and inconvenience required to re-list the property several times. All my Clients really appreciate this easy, simple, straightforward way of doing business.

I can't help but wonder at times, when we get to debating all those complex agency issues and the other issues that are forever haunting our industry, if it isn't all because we've made doing business much more difficult than it really needs to be.

MOST CANCELLATIONS
AT MY OWN INSTIGATION

I carry more than fifty listings at all times and since implementing my "cancel anytime" policy I've had no more than one or two cancellations per year. More often than not the cancellations are at my instigation, not the Sellers'.

In the case of the odd one I do cancel, the cancellation doesn't usually take place until we're into what would have been the second or third semester, if I'd taken the listing for the minimum sixty days required by our local board. So I really haven't lost anything anyway.

EFFECTIVE
USE OF TIME

There isn't a more effective way of using your time than writing listings for a long term. It often takes more than 90 days to sell properly priced listings in our area. If I wrote the more than fifty listings I carry for only two months at a time instead of six months to a year, and assuming I'd only have to spend an hour on each re-listing, I'd be spending as many as 300 hours, or up to one full month of my time yearly, doing nothing but re-listing expires.

As you and I both know, it's never a matter of simply getting a listing re-signed. You have to sell the Client on everything all over again. That usually takes more than an hour. It clearly pays dividends to give cancellation privileges and write your listings for a longer term.

CHAPTER 15

SHOULD YOU BE FIRST, LAST, OR IN BETWEEN?

Whether one should be first, last or in between, if a

Seller plans to interview several Agents before deciding who to list with, is a negotiating point that generates endless discussion among Real Estate Salespeople. For me it's easy. I want to be first, or next, if someone has already been there.

LAST IN GETS
THE "BOOBY-PRIZE"

I hear arguments made all the time on the advantages of being last. I can't for the life of me understand that kind of reasoning. As far as I'm concerned the person who comes in last wins the "booby-prize".

My competitors can be sure of one thing. If they let me go first, their appointment will get canceled. I'm going to write the listing while I'm there. It's that simple! In this regard I'd like to share a little negotiating technique with you that has worked wonders for me over the years.

APPOINTMENT
CANCELLATION TECHNIQUE

I call this my "appointment cancellation technique". It eliminates one of the biggest obstacles Salespeople encounter to writing a listing at the time of making a Listing Presentation, when the Seller has made appointments to interview several Agents.

Provided we asked the proper qualifying questions at the time of contact, we usually know in advance of going to do the Presentation, that this is what the Seller plans on doing. However, even the best of us get fooled occasionally, and we don't find out until we've done our Presentation that the Seller has made appointments with other Agents as well as us.

EFFECTIVE AFTER PRESENTATION ONLY

In either case this technique will be effective, but only after you've made your Presentation. If the Seller informs me before I make my Presentation that he intends to interview other Agents, I simply carry on and make my Presentation as though I didn't expect anything different. Since I always use the assumptive approach, after I've made my Presentation I just begin filling in the contract. If the subject is going to come up it'll come up at that time.

I'LL CANCEL THOSE APPOINTMENTS FOR YOU

The Seller might say, "Marilyn, I'd like to give you the listing but I can't. I've made appointments with two other Agents to come and talk with us. I even promised one of them he could come last and I wouldn't list with anyone until I heard what he had to say."

My response would be, "Don't worry about that. I'll cancel those appointments for you." I go on to say, "You probably called those who you thought were the three best Salespeople in the city to come and meet with you, right?" Of course they did. They certainly didn't call the three worst.

Then I continue and say, "Think about this. You're going to have two other top Salespeople come and spend two hours of their time with you going over all the same material and statistics I've just covered. Then you're going to call me back to list your home. You're going to have a couple of the best Salespeople in town a little bit miffed because you didn't give them the listing. They'll probably be less than excited about selling your home."

"I'll cancel those appointments for you; I'll give them all the information about your listing before anyone else knows about it; I'll get them excited about working with me to get your home sold and on top of that they'll be happy you didn't waste their time."

STRONG LISTING PRESENTATION NEEDED

Provided you have a strong Listing Presentation to back it up, this technique will work nearly every time. If you don't have a strong Listing Presentation you probably won't get the listing no matter what technique you use!

In fact, when competing with other Agents if you don't have a strong Listing Presentation, you probably won't get the listing no matter what order you get to make your Presentation in.

GET CONTROL OF YOUR DESTINY

The one thing I do know is this — the sooner I get to make my Listing Presentation, the sooner I can eliminate the competition and get myself in control. These after all, are the two most important things you accomplish by writing a listing. Having more listings than other Salespeople in your area means you have less competition and more control over both the market and your own destiny than they have.

BECOME EXPERT AT NEGOTIATING WITH SELLERS

Good Listers never find themselves in a slump, no matter what kind of market exists. They don't know what the word means. They're **"slump proof"**. I learned a long time ago that having more listings is the **"cure"** for virtually every problem the real estate market can place in the way of a Real Estate Agent!

In order to get your share of the listings available in your area, it's vitally important to become an expert at negotiating with Sellers.

CHAPTER 16

CREATING
DEADLINES

Another effective negotiating technique is to create

deadlines. They play a vitally important role in the negotiating process.

CREATE A DEADLINE
— CAUSE AN ACTION

Deadlines are limitations on the use of time, that require a person to act or not to act, on or before a specific date or time. It's interesting to note that several surveys have shown that the excuse most frequently used by procrastinators who fail to complete assignments in a timely manner is: **"No Deadline was Specified"**.

In reality, our daily lives are governed by deadlines. They usually require us to take some form of action and we respond marvelously well. They inspire people to get things done.

Meeting deadlines is something we learn about at an early age. Children have to be in bed by a certain time. There's a deadline by which they have to be at school. Homework and assignments have to be done on time. They have to be home for dinner at six o'clock. Then there's that thing called curfew. And on it goes.

DEADLINES
ENCOURAGE COMMUNICATION

By the time we're adults meeting deadlines has become second nature to us. We take deadlines seriously. We're constantly striving to meet them. Our utility bills are a good example of this. They have to be paid by a certain date. In response to that deadline we take an action. We either pay the bill or we negotiate an extension of time for its payment.

In the latter case, to negotiate an extension of the payment deadline, we have to communicate with the Utility Company. So not only do deadlines cause people to take action, but they also encourage communication. That's why creating deadlines is such an effective negotiating technique.

USE DEADLINES
CREATIVELY

There are numerous opportunities for Real Estate Salespeople to use deadlines creatively, to assist us in the negotiating process. When doing a Listing Agreement, for example, you can establish deadlines by which the price will be reduced by specific increments if the property hasn't sold. Failing that, you can establish deadlines to discuss price reductions. You can set deadlines by which to implement other marketing strategies, such as higher commissions or bonuses to encourage interest in the property by a wider circle of Salespeople.

You can host a progressive dinner with other Agents who have listings in the same area, to hold a number of homes open for viewing by other Salespeople on a certain date. You can use this date as a deadline to discuss a price reduction with your Seller so his home will be the most attractively priced on the tour.

You can use the date you send out your monthly or bi-weekly "Hot Sheets" to the top Agents in the area, as a deadline for discussing price reductions, increased commissions and bonuses or all three together. The opportunities are endless.

USE DEADLINES IMPOSED BY OTHERS

In many cases deadlines imposed by other sources give us tremendous leverage when negotiating with both Buyers and Sellers. In the case of corporate transfers for example, there may be deadlines imposed by the Clients' company. They may have given him a four day expense paid trip to your city in order to buy a home. Take two days off for travel and he has two days in which to buy. Wouldn't you like to have hundreds of Clients who have only two days to buy?

Perhaps the Client has built a new home or sold his present home and has to move by a certain date. Smart negotiators ask the right questions to determine the deadlines imposed by other sources. Then they use these deadlines to their advantage in the negotiating process.

Remember, deadlines cause people to take action and they also encourage communication. That's why expert negotiators always determine what deadlines have been imposed by others, and are always looking for opportunities to impose deadlines on the other side themselves. So be creative. Impose deadlines whenever you can. Take advantage of them to assist you in the negotiating process.

CHAPTER 17

PROSPECTING
TO WIN

Mention the word prospecting, and Salespeople

immediately think it means asking people to give them the names of anybody else who needs their services at this very moment. If by chance the Buyer or Seller knows of someone at the time, the Salesperson will probably get that person's name and phone number.

Because of the way we're trained, the logical extension of this process is to ask the Buyer or Seller to refer their friends and acquaintances to us, if and when they have a need for the services we provide.

WHAT
STUDIES REVEAL

Several studies and surveys about this subject confirm that Buyers and Sellers will do repeat and referral business with a Real Estate Salesperson on a consistent basis, as long as they consider the relationship to be mutually beneficial. When it comes to Sellers, these same studies show that the vast majority of referrals are received during the active listing period and shortly afterwards. In the case of Buyers the vast majority of referrals are received during the period between the date they buy a home and the closing date, and shortly thereafter.

What do these studies tell us? First of all, the majority of referrals are received during the period when the Salesperson is negotiating with the party about buying or selling a home or shortly thereafter.

In other words, most referrals are received during or immediately following that period when a Salesperson has the most frequent contact with his Buyer or Seller — the same period when the relationship is perceived by both parties to be a win-win situation.

But these studies tell us something else, don't they? In

view of the above, what do you think would happen if Salespeople maintained that same kind of frequent contact with Buyers and Sellers, and continued to demonstrate the mutual value of the relationship, after the sale or purchase of a home? Do you think they'd get more referrals from their Clients and Customers? More repeat business? On an ongoing basis even? The answer is obvious, isn't it!

REPEAT AND
REFERRAL AQUIFER

When we've been in this business for a while, we have at our disposal a tremendous pool of the absolute best prospects in the world — those Clients and Customers who have already dealt with us. I liken these people to a huge aquifer of the freshest, purest water available anywhere, into which a well has been drilled and a pump has been attached.

If no one visits the well and the pump isn't used frequently it loses its prime. Before it will deliver more water someone has to prime it. The longer it's left on its own the harder it is to prime. If it's abandoned for a long period of time the leathers dry out and before it will deliver water again some repairs might be necessary.

KEEP REPEAT AND
REFERRAL PUMP PRIMED

So it is with our repeat and referral aquifer. We have to visit the well regularly, to prospect the aquifer and keep the pump primed. If we do that, the pump will deliver plenty of repeat and referral business to us. If we visit the well infrequently, we'll have to prime the pump before it delivers. If we abandon the well for a long time, the pump will need some fixing before it will start producing again.

As part of my ongoing personal promotion program, when a prospect has been referred by someone else, I keep the pump primed by immediately sending out an appropriate letter of appreciation. I thank them for the referral and make a subtle solicitation for more referrals. I notify them again when I've completed a transaction with the referral, say thank you once more and make a subtle solicitation once again for more referrals.

THANK ORIGINAL SOURCE OFTEN

When a Client or Customer who has dealt with me before calls to do business with me again, I know why they've called me. But I don't just leave it at that. I look up the source from which they originally came to me, and if they were referred to me by someone else, I send a letter to the person who originally referred them to me. I tell him they are dealing with me again and say thank you once more for the original referral. You'd be surprised how often this primes a pump that's been dormant for a while and results in another referral or two coming my way.

So, go to the well often. Keep the pump primed by prospecting the acquifer of Clients and Customers who've already dealt with you. Provided you've given them outstanding service in the first place, you can significantly increase your volume of repeat and referral business by maintaining frequent contact with your existing Clients and Customers.

Provide them with regular market updates. Be genuinely interested in them as people. Show sincere appreciation for their assistance in helping you achieve your goals. They'll recognize the win-win benefits of the relationship, and they'll respond to your prospecting by continuing to deal with you themselves and by referring others to you as well.

A GOLDEN
OPPORTUNITY

At the conclusion of a Listing Presentation Real Estate Salespeople have a tremendous opportunity to do some win-win prospecting. It's unfortunate but true, that this opportunity is hardly ever taken advantage of. In fact it's much more than a simple run of the mill opportunity. If ever there was such a thing as a golden opportunity this is it. Yet for some reason that I can't understand for the life of me, it gets totally overlooked or under utilized in the vast majority of cases.

If Salespeople took full and proper advantage of this opportunity, they could have anywhere from a few hundred to a few thousand prime quality prospects to work with at all times, depending on the number of active listings they carry. There'd be little need to expend the huge amounts of time, energy and money that many do, on such low return activities as direct mailings and telemarketing to the masses out there, with whom they have nothing in common.

PROSPECT AND
TRAIN BEFORE LEAVING

After a listing agreement is signed by the Seller, one of

the last things I do before leaving is a little prospecting. I begin by using the traditional approach and I talk to them about whether they know of anyone else thinking of selling or buying.

I spend a little time training them to sell me. I tell them what my goals are; that I really need their help to reach these goals and I'll really appreciate them referring others to me. I give them some of my personal brochures to pass out to friends, relatives or acquaintances who may need my services in the future.

WIN-WIN
APPROACH

After each Listing Agreement is signed I give my Sellers three pages of Sellers' Homework to complete. They are printed for your own use on the following three pages.

The first two have nothing to do with prospecting, but I'm including them because they'll save you hours and hours of time. For years now, neither I nor my assistant have had to spend any time preparing the copy for the feature sheets or brochures we use to promote my listings. The Sellers do that for us when they complete the first two pages of Sellers' Homework.

In any event, it's the third page of Sellers' Homework that we're concerned with here. So let's take a look at it now, before we proceed. As you can see, it's a simple form titled "Sellers' Friends and Acquaintances" that's divided into three columns, one each for names, addresses and phone numbers. I tell them I want them to give me the names, addresses and phone numbers for a minimum of 50 friends and acquaintances.

Seller's Homework

Page 1

Have You Supplied Us With:
❑ A Key ❑ Survey Certificate ❑ Mortgage Number # _____

Here are the things we think are great about our neighborhood:

Information about our neighbors: (such as ages and number of children in the area)

Here are the things about our home we think a purchaser would like to know about:

Exterior	
Interior	Living Room
	Dining Room
	Kitchen

Here are the things about our home we think a purchaser would like to know about *(continued)*:

Interior	Family Room
	Laundry Room
	Bathrooms
	Master Bedroom
	Additional Bedrooms
	Basement
	Additional Rooms and Information

Our Average Utility Bills Are: *(A range is OK)*

Electric	Water & Sewer
Gas	Lake Fees *(If applicable)*

Seller's Homework

Sellers' Friends and Acquaintances *(50 minimum)*		
Name	**Address**	**Phone #s**

WHAT'S
IN IT FOR THEM?

Before people will give you this type of list, there has to be something in it for them. So I tell them what I'm going to do with the list. When I do, they get downright excited about the idea.

I explain that I'm going to send a letter to everyone on their list, telling them I have the home listed for sale, and asking each of them if they know of anyone looking for a home who might be interested in buying it.

I point out that all of these people know a whole different circle of friends and acquaintances, any of whom might know someone who'd be interested in their home. I show them a copy of the letter I'll be sending out. I emphasize strongly that this is a superb marketing tool, and that often this is how I find Buyers for my listings.

The first time I used this idea I couldn't believe what happened. When my assistant picked up the list, two days later there was almost 150 names on it. In addition to a list of friends and acquaintances they photo-copied their church list, their golf list and their curling club list for me. The ironic thing was that I sold the home to an employee of one of the people on their curling club list.

WHO
THEY KNOW

When you ask people for a list of 50 names, usually their initial reaction is, they won't be able to come up with that many. Yet, it's estimated that the average person knows between 175 and 200 people. These include relatives and friends; social, religious, business, educational and recreational acquaintances.

I can't emphasize strongly enough how important it is to point out the various categories they can draw names from. It's not unusual to get lists of over a hundred names from Sellers, provided you have such a discussion with them.

WHAT HAVE
WE GOT HERE

Think about what you get here — the names, addresses and phone numbers of 50 to 150 or more people with whom you know someone in common. When you write them, enclose your personal brochure or scratch pad or other propaganda with your picture on it. Then follow up with a phone call to see if they got your letter, and find out if they know anyone who might be interested in their friends' home.

They'll often say, "Oh, we didn't know the Sellers were moving. Where are they moving to?" What an easy conversation. You both know the same person. What a great way to prospect! You can follow up as often as you like to try to make Clients out of them.

There's never a shortage of reasons to call these people back or send them additional information. When you sell the home, phone or write them all again and give them the Seller's new address. A few weeks later send them another brochure or scratch pad and give them their new business phone number. Call them again with the Seller's new residence phone numbers and so on. By this time you'll actually be dealing with some of the people on the list.

TRAIN BUYERS
TO SELL YOU

When it comes to prospecting, one of the most consistent mistakes we make as Real Estate Salespeople is that we ask for help and then fail to tell people how they can help us. It's simply not good enough to just ask for help! You have to tell people how they can help you! In other words you have to train them to sell you!

For example, let's take a look at what happens when we sell someone a home. At some time during the process, provided we've done a good job, our Buyers tell us how happy they are with our services. When this happens I always tell them I'll really appreciate any help they can give me. They nearly always say, "Marilyn we'd never even think of dealing with anyone else".

They think that yes, if they decide to sell again in 10 years, they'll definitely call us. But that's as far as the public thinks! So I seize this opportunity to do a bit of training!

I tell them I appreciate the fact they won't deal with anyone else, but I need more than that from them. I tell them what my goals are and that I'd really like them to be a part of helping me achieve them. I tell them I'm going to send a supply of my personal brochures to their places of business, and that every time they hear the words, "Real Estate", I want them to tell the party about me and give them one of my brochures.

It's vitally important to send these brochures along with an appropriate letter to both their places of business — **never to their home.** If you send them to their home they will get stuffed in a drawer or thrown out. After all, it's at their office or place of business, where they have most of their people contact.

NEGOTIATING AT ITS VERY BEST!

People love to share and participate in exciting events, but outside of political campaigns they're seldom given an opportunity to share in making someone else successful.

Tell your Clients and Customers what your goals are — that you want to be #1 in your office or city or board or state or province, or whatever your goal is. Tell them that not only will you appreciate their help — but you need it. Then explain what they can do to help you succeed. Give them the opportunity to contribute to your success, and you'll be amazed at how enthusiastically they'll respond.

Real Estate Salespeople who become experts at **negotiating with** Buyers and Sellers always have more prospects to work with than they can handle effectively. Prospecting your Clients and Customers for new business is negotiating of the highest order.

Become an expert at negotiating with Sellers and you'll get a list of at least 50 names every time you write a listing. Provided you carry enough listings, you'll always have from several hundred to several thousand high quality prospects to work with. Add to this the prospects your Sellers and Buyers will refer to you because you've trained them to sell you and you'll be the busiest Salesperson in your area!

Prospects referred to you by those who have already dealt with you, are the easiest people in the world to deal with because they already have considerable faith and trust in you.

Prospecting to win is negotiating at its very best!

SECTION THREE

NEGOTIATING
WITH BUYERS

CHAPTER 18

THE BUYER INTERVIEW — A
POWERFUL NEGOTIATING TOOL

One of the most powerful negotiating tools that I've

had at my disposal as a Real Estate Salesperson is the "Buyer Interview". It enables me to sell Buyers the first day we go out looking at homes. Rarely does it go beyond the second day.

Before I started doing Buyer Interviews I simply reacted to phone calls. I'd run off and meet Buyers in restaurants, parking lots, or in front of a property. I wouldn't do that today for the world. The only way I'll show a prospect a property today, is if the prospect first comes to my office for a thorough Buyer Interview.

MAIN PURPOSES
OF BUYER INTERVIEW

There are five main purposes for doing a Buyer Interview. From a negotiating perspective each one is as important as the other, and they are as follows:

1. To sell yourself;
2. To qualify the Buyer financially;
3. To gain knowledge of the wants, needs and lifestyle of the Buyer;
4. To alleviate any doubts and concerns the Buyer may have about buying real estate or dealing with a Real Estate Agent;
5. To get a pledge of loyalty.

The Interview procedure takes between an hour and a half and two hours. We discuss their potential purchase in detail. At the conclusion they engage me as their exclusive personal Real Estate Agent, just as they'd engage the services of an attorney or any other professional.

The interview that I conduct with every Buyer I work with consists of 17 steps. Each step deals with issues that are critical to their home purchase. The bottom line is that at the conclusion of my Buyer Interview, depending on the form of representation we agree on, I have a loyal Customer or Client who'll deal only with me, and who'll usually buy the first or second day out looking at homes.

During the Interview I condition my Buyers to give me a fair offer on any home they try to buy. They nearly always do. As a result of this, at Offer Presentation time I can go into negotiations from a position of power with a "You-Gotta-Believe" attitude and say, "I've got a really good offer for you". I can then proceed to present it like I really mean what I say. Because of this I seldom fail to get an acceptable deal negotiated. The "Buyer Interview" is a crucial part of the negotiating process in every sale I make.

UNPRODUCTIVE
USE OF TIME

As stated above, I never show a property to anyone, including people who have bought through me before, unless they first come to my office for a "Buyer Interview". As far as I'm concerned there isn't a more unproductive way for Salespeople to spend their time, than to show properties to prospects with whom they haven't first done a thorough "Buyer Interview".

Here's why!

For several years now I've been referring between 20 and 30 sign call prospects per week to other Agents. If they sell the prospect the home they call on or any other home, I get a 25% referral fee. These are prospects who won't come for an Interview.

Since starting to follow this procedure, I've never needed more than the fingers on one hand to count the number of referral fees I've received from this source, during an entire year. If they wouldn't come for a Buyer Interview they simply weren't Buyers. If that doesn't prove the value and common sense of not showing property to a prospect unless they first come for a "Buyer Interview", I don't know what does.

LET'S DO
A LITTLE MATH

In case you're still not convinced, let's do a little math here. I gave away between 20 and 30 sign calls weekly on the basis that I'd get a 25% referral fee if the Salesperson sold the Prospect the property they called on or any other property. That works out to roughly 1300 sign calls per year, that other Agents chased after and the most they've ever sold is five. If they spent only an hour and a half on each showing, that means they spent 1950 hours per year, chasing after prospects who hardly ever buy.

Let's relate this to my situation. For the past several years, I've sold over 200 properties each year and worked only six months of the year doing so. Based on a 12 hour work day I was working roughly 1950 hours each year.

That's about the same number of hours other Agents spent, showing property to the sign call prospects I referred to them. But here's the interesting thing. If I'd chased these sign calls myself rather than give them away, I wouldn't have had time to write a single listing and I'd have sold 5 or less homes in a year instead of over 200 like I did consistently for a long number of years.

I'm not going to deal with each step of the Buyer Interview in detail here. There is a step-by-step discussion of the Buyer Interview in my earlier book, *Championship Selling*. It's also recorded on one of my audio cassette albums. Both of these are available from MCJ Publishing Ltd. There is an order form for these in the back of this book, for anyone who's interested.

However, I am going to deal with one of the steps here, because it's such a vital step when negotiating with Buyers — a vital step that will enable you to sell Buyers faster and use your time far more productively.

PLAY THE NAME GAME

In step #16 of the Interview I explain the procedure we'll be using when we look at homes. I tell them we're going to make their home buying easy and we're also going to make it fun.

I explain that I'll be getting them to do two things as we look at homes. The first is that I'll get them to play what I call the "Name Game". After we look at each home and get back to the car I'll want them to give each home a silly or distinctive name. The sillier the name is the better.

EASIER TO REMEMBER

Aside from adding an element of fun while we're looking at homes, at the end of the tour we'll have no trouble remembering which house we're referring to. It's far easier and less confusing to remember what a house is like, if you refer to it by a silly or distinctive name, than it is to remember it by address.

It gets really funny at times as people debate the merits of one name over another. Sometimes they have their kids with them and the whole family gets involved. Some people have great imaginations and have no trouble coming up with really distinctive names.

Others have no imagination and in those cases you have to help them out a bit. If they really like some feature about the home, I'll suggest they use their own descriptive adjective as the name. If for example, when we walk into a certain house they see an aquarium in the wall and say, "Aren't those fish beautiful!", when we get back to the car I'll suggest they name that house, "The Fish Hatchery".

I've had people buy homes with some interesting names over the years. I've got people living in the Outhouse; others who live in the Pig Stye, and I'm probably the only Saleslady in the world who's got Buyers living in Buckingham Palace. This house had pictures of the Royal Family hanging in every room. There was even one hanging above the throne in the bathroom.

RATING
THE HOMES

The second thing I'll be getting them to do is rate the homes as we view them. I want them to rate them according to choice, I.E., first, second and third choice, with number one being the best. In other words they'll be keeping a consideration list as they view the homes.

However, they're only allowed to keep their three top choices on the consideration list at any time. No more!

SOMEBODY GETS BUMPED

That means that once we've looked at the fourth house, somebody has to get bumped. From then on every time we look at a house they have to make a decision about whether that house bumps one of the others off the list or not. Once a property gets bumped from the list, it never gets mentioned or thought about again — ever. That's the rule!

Another rule is, we will never leave the driveway of the house we've just viewed until it's been both **named** and **rated**. It doesn't matter how long it takes. It often takes 20 minutes or longer to decide which house remains on the list.

If my driver Terry, notices we're going to be late for the next appointment he never interrupts me. He knows how important this exercise is. He quietly picks up the phone, calls ahead, explains we're running a little late, and confirms we'll still be coming.

Like most Salespeople I know, for years I ran with Buyers from one house to the next and the next and the next, without having them rate the homes as we went. If you're presently showing homes that way, I can tell you from experience that at the end of the day, more often than not, you've converted someone who started out as a motivated Buyer into a confused looker.

The truth of the matter is that Salespeople make confused lookers out of highly motivated Buyers all the time, without even realizing it. Then they have the nerve to blame the Buyers for being nothing but lookers and complain about them wasting their time. I did the same thing for years. Doing a 17 step Buyer Interview and having my Buyers play the "Name and Rate Game" has changed all that. I now sell most of my Buyers the first or second day out. It's rare that it goes beyond the second day.

THREE
SIGNIFICANT PURPOSES

The process of naming and rating homes as we view them serves three significant purposes. Firstly, it keeps the Buyers focused on their three top choices at all times throughout the tour. That after all, is absolutely essential if we're going to conclude a transaction quickly. If we can't get our Buyers focused they're never going to buy in one or two days.

The second thing it does is even more important. It gets them making definite decisions. That too, is what we have to get them doing, if we want to conclude a transaction quickly. Like getting our Buyers focused, if we can't get them making definite decisions they're never going to buy in one or two days.

Thirdly, it gives me some crystal clear insight into what they really want. That's also important if we're going to conclude a transaction quickly. I like to say it let's me see through their eyes.

If you sit in the driveway for up to 20 minutes or longer, and listen carefully as your Buyers weigh one house against another, believe me you'll have a crystal clear picture of what they really want. If you haven't found the right home the first day out, you won't have any trouble zeroing in on it the second day.

A
SECOND LOOK

I tell them at the end of the tour we'll go back and have a second look at their first choice. If I'm smart enough to figure out which home they're going to like the best before we go out looking, I'll show it first every time. If it keeps winning as they compare it to each of the other homes on the tour, it builds up more and more in their minds. Quite often we can do an offer when we go back for that second look.

The Buyer Interview is a powerful negotiating tool, to say nothing about its effectiveness in the area of time management. Like I've already said, most of the people I deal with buy the first or second day out. Rarely does it go beyond the second day. I'd never be able to do this without first doing a thorough Buyer Interview and preparing my Buyers properly in advance.

INCIDENT
WITH A LESSON

The reason I started doing Buyer Interviews was because of an incident that happened when I was in my mid-twenties and still fairly new to the business. I was on floor duty in the office and received a call from this lovely sounding lady. She wanted to see another firms' listing, on the opposite side of town from where she lived. She told me she called our firm because of its good reputation.

Being new to the business, I asked her a couple of really tough qualifying questions — like her name and address. I phoned the Seller, made an appointment and picked her up at her apartment.

On the way over she told me how she was recently widowed and would be buying for all cash with the proceeds from her late husband's insurance policy. She was really hoping she'd like the home, because her sister lived nearby and she really liked the area. When she viewed the home she really liked it. She told me she was going around the corner to visit her sister and discuss making an offer with her. She said she'd get back to me shortly.

As I drove back to the office I was on cloud nine. I was sure I had a deal. When I got back there was a phone call for me from the Listing Agent. His Seller had called him and told him that he'd shown the home to the same lady a couple of days before. Exactly the same thing had happened to him when he showed her the home.

We were both a little bit suspicious. After doing a little detective work we found out this lady was actually on city welfare. She couldn't afford a free lunch let alone a home, and we'd both been duped into providing free taxi service to this lady, so she could visit her sister on the other side of town. I'd be willing to bet that some other innocent Salesperson drove her home under the same pretense.

That incident caused me to start doing Buyer Interviews before I showed a property to anyone. The Interview I did in those days wasn't nearly as thorough as the one I do today, but making that decision was one of the most important steps I took towards negotiating the use of my time more efficiently and effectively. It made me realize that time is a precious commodity, that shouldn't be squandered on poor quality prospects about whom we know virtually nothing.

GET
EYEBALL TO EYEBALL

Studies show that super achievers and top producers in the real estate industry, spend between 80 and 90% of their working time eyeball to eyeball, negotiating with a prospect who is a potential Buyer or Seller.

If we want to be more successful as Salespeople, we have to get ourselves in a position where we're spending more time negotiating transactions with Buyers and Sellers, and less time spinning our wheels.

That's what the Buyer Interview does. It enables Real Estate Salespeople and Brokers to spend more of their time negotiating transactions on behalf of people who are really Buyers, instead of acting as a tour guide for people who seldom buy, or aren't Buyers at all. That's what it did for me! It will do the same for you!

Whether you're into Traditional Brokerage or Buyer Brokerage, it makes no difference. The Buyer Interview is one of the most powerful negotiating tools we have at our disposal — all we have to do is use it!

CHAPTER 19

SETTING
THE STAGE

Whether your Client is the Seller or the Buyer, be

sure to put the other Agent at ease when you set up the appointment to present an offer. You can usually set the tone of the negotiations at this stage. Tell the other Agent you look forward to working with them to put a deal together that will be fair and equitable to everyone involved.

If it's his offer, tell him if it's decent you'll do your best to make it work; that you'll treat him with respect and you expect the same in return. If it's his listing and your offer, tell him you'll do everything possible to make him look good to his Seller. If he's inexperienced, untrained or simply has an ego problem, this will dispel any fears he has that he'll look bad to his Seller. He won't feel he has to take issue with every point in your offer, just to make himself look good during the Presentation.

SOME
<u>GROUND RULES</u>

I always tell the other Agent I will not cut my commission for any reason or for any amount, regardless of how small that amount may be. I don't want that to become part of the negotiations, under any circumstances. I also tell them, especially when I'm representing the Buyer, I'd like to present my offer and then I'd like both of us to sit silent until the Seller responds, no matter how long it takes the Seller to do so. If it takes 15 minutes or half an hour even — that's O.K. If nothing else, my 30 years of experience negotiating offers has proven beyond a doubt that, "He who speaks first loses".

On occasion other Salespeople tell me they won't go along with this suggestion, for one reason or another. If that happens, it's OK with me. It's their decision and I respect it. In fact it usually works to their detriment and consequently to my advantage.

The reality is that it's next to impossible for any Real Estate Salesperson to negotiate properly on behalf of their Seller until they know exactly what his objections to the Offer really are. Over the years, I've witnessed some pretty embarrassing situations for other Salespeople when they took it upon themselves to decide what the Seller didn't like about an Offer, only to have the Seller take rather obvious exception to what the Salesperson was doing.

When I know in advance that other Salespeople are going to take this position, I present my Offer and then sit back and enjoy the show. They and their Clients provide me with all kinds of valuable information while airing their differences, prior to getting around to what their objections to the Offer really are.

When I'm satisfied I've got all the information I can get I proceed to isolate the objections and close the deal.

AVOID
OUT FRONT MEETINGS

Never discuss the terms of the offer with the other Agent before Presentation. And since you want to develop an atmosphere of trust with the Seller, don't meet the Agent out front before going in to present the offer. Deal after deal is lost because Sellers see the Agents meeting out front and wonder what on earth they're cooking up out there. Having a meeting with the other Agent on the doorstep before you go in to present an offer, looks both suspicious and unprofessional. It should be avoided at all costs.

PRESENT OFFERS
IN THE OFFICE

When there's an offer to be presented, if it's your listing have the Seller come to your office and do the Presentation there. When it's your offer and another Agent's listing, try and get them to have the Seller meet you both at the Listing Agent's office.

Whenever possible bring your Buyer with you so counter-offers can be dealt with on the spot. I'm not suggesting, nor would I ever recommend, getting Buyers and Sellers together. Simply arrange an office to accommodate you and your Buyer at the Lister's premises. Then you and the Lister can simply go from office to office with counter-offers till you complete a transaction.

When another Salesperson has an offer on your listing, invite him to bring his Buyers with him and provide them with an office at your premises. I've used this procedure to present offers for several years now.

On numerous occasions the other Salesperson has asked me to explain our position to his Buyers in order to close a sale. If he was running in the usual manner, from my Sellers' home to his Buyers' location with counter-offers, this couldn't happen. In that situation, I would not get an opportunity to meet and speak with his Buyers. There simply isn't a more efficient way of doing business, nor a better way of maintaining control of the Offer Presentation process.

I know it's not always possible to do this, but on most occasions it's easy to accomplish. However, it will simply not happen at all if you don't ask your Sellers to do so, or if you don't suggest it to the Lister when you call for an appointment.

During every Listing Presentation, I make my Sellers aware this is the procedure we'll follow when we get an offer. When I explain the reasons for doing so there's never a problem. In fact I've had numerous Sellers say they couldn't understand why all real estate transactions aren't conducted that way.

SEVERAL
COMPELLING REASONS

Presenting offers at the office eliminates doorstep meetings with other Agents and from a negotiating perspective there are several compelling reasons for using this procedure, if at all possible.

First of all, negotiations are always easier to conduct and are far more productive when conducted in a relaxed and business-like atmosphere away from the distractions of everyday life.

How many times have you been in the middle of presenting an offer in someone's home when the kids got into an argument, or the phone rang, or the TV was blaring in the background, or the dog freaked out, or any number of other distractions occurred that required the Seller's attention. The absolute worst situation is when friends or relatives drop by for a visit and get involved in the offer.

Having the Seller come to the office eliminates all these distractions and permits the Seller to give his undivided attention to dealing with the offer.

SELLERS RESPECT
PROCESS MORE

The fact is, Sellers have far more respect for the whole process when they come to the office for the Presentation of an offer. After all is said and done that's the way it should be. Selling a home is serious business. It's usually the largest asset disposition your Seller ever makes.

Using this procedure makes you look far more professional. It puts you on the same level as other professionals who end up being participants in real estate transactions, such as lawyers, bankers, title companies and tax advisors, whose Clients come to their offices to transact business.

Obviously using this procedure makes eminent good sense from a time-management perspective as well. Think about it! While they're driving to your office and home again you can accomplish something productive.

CHAPTER 20

NEVER KNOCK
THE SELLERS' HOME

If it's your offer, never knock the Seller's home.

Nothing makes a Real Estate Salesperson look more ridiculous, than to show up with a list of things that are wrong with a home, to try and convince a Seller to accept a low-ball offer. I've watched Agents stumble and stammer and embarrass themselves right out of a deal, as they tried to convince my Seller the only reason he had an offer at all, was because they were such hot shot Salespeople.

According to them they were somehow able to prevail over their all powerful Buyer and get an offer on our lowly listing. The truth of the matter is that when Salespeople use this approach, they come across as weaklings, who've been intimidated by a Buyer who was able to manipulate them at will. Sellers then respond accordingly.

A
TYPICAL CASE

A few years ago, I had a Salesperson show up with an offer on one of my listings. He had a list of 14 items that according to him had to be corrected to make the property worth what we were asking for it.

We had three appraisals on the property to back up our price, plus a Home-Alize inspection that indicated the home was in excellent repair. My Sellers' company had these done because they were taking the home over quickly, having transferred my Seller out of the country on real short notice.

We signed the offer back and sent the embarrassed Salesman on his way with copies of the Home-Alize report, that indicated there was definitely nothing wrong with the home. We also gave him copies of the three appraisals which clearly substantiated our listing price.

The ironic thing was, one of the appraisals was done by the appraisal division of his own company. I'll never forget the look on his face when my Seller asked him whether he didn't know what he was talking about, or if his company was in the habit of charging fees for doing false property appraisals. Needless to say we never heard from him again.

TWO FATAL
NEGOTIATING MISTAKES

That Agent made two fatal negotiating mistakes. First, you should never run down a Sellers' home, because there's really a lot of each of us in our homes. That means when you knock someone's home you're knocking them. If you start off by pointing out all the things the Buyer doesn't like about the home, the Seller will simply get his back up, and if anything, will be less than sympathetic to your position. If you want to make a deal you need him on your side — not against you.

MY BUYERS
LOVE YOUR HOME

Before I present an offer I tell the Sellers that my Buyers love their home. That makes sense. After all they're trying to buy it! Let's face it, they wouldn't be doing so if they hated it! Even if they were buying it for the lot value only, they'd still be buying because they liked it. Then I tell them how nice my Buyers are, why the neighborhood is perfect for them, and how the home lends itself perfectly to their lifestyle.

And you know something interesting? Homes often sell because the most important thing to the Seller is that the home sells to someone they like. If you want the Seller to like your Buyer, all you have to do is tell the Seller how much your Buyer likes their home — which is so much a part of them.

YOU CAN'T
WING IT AND WIN

The other fatal mistake that the Agent made was that he wasn't properly prepared for the negotiations he was trying to undertake. Believe me, being properly prepared is a prime requisite for successful negotiating. You can't "Wing It and Win". The better prepared you are — the more thorough your preparation is — the more likely you are to reach an agreement. Hasty decisions about the tactics you're going to use will usually prove to be bad decisions.

If that Salesman had simply called me beforehand, I could have told him we had three appraisals and a Home-Alize inspection. I could have told him as well that one of the appraisals were done by his own company and given him copies in advance.

They might have helped him write a decent offer, or may have prevented him bringing us an offer at all, which would have been better than what he brought us. At the very least he wouldn't have been in the embarrassing position he found himself in as a result of not being properly prepared.

USE THE
"NICE GUY" APPROACH

Before you write an offer speak with the other Agent if possible. Use the "Nice Guy" approach to find out as much as you can about his Clients; their reasons for selling, their goals, their commitments and so on.

Assure them you want to be fair, and your objective is to try and make a deal that everyone will be happy with. Ask him how he as a Real Estate Professional like yourself, really feels about the property; the price, what the Seller might take, if the drapes and appliances are negotiable items and how important the possession date might be to the Seller.

If you get some idea of where the other side is coming from, you can determine with your Buyer what strategy you should use to accomplish your goals.

We have to keep in mind however, that it might not be prudent to base your entire strategy on what the other Agent tells you. It's always wise to remember that Sellers often have a different opinion than the Agent has about some things.

SELLERS ARE
NICE, DECENT PEOPLE

It's also important during negotiations to tell your Buyers that the Sellers are really nice, decent people. I remember the first home we bought. The Saleslady kept telling us what jerks the Sellers were. We believed her, and during the process of making the deal we got our backs up considerably against the Sellers whom we'd never met.

One of the items that nearly caused us not to go ahead with the purchase, was the refusal of the Seller to include the appliances. Between the date they accepted the offer and the closing date, the Sellers invited us up to show us where the water shutoff valves and things like that were located.

When we got there we got the biggest surprise of our lives. We couldn't believe it. The Sellers were the nicest people you'd ever want to meet. They didn't fit the Saleslady's description in the slightest.

Before we left they told us that since we were such a nice young couple just starting out in life; who'd borrowed the down payment and closing costs from our in-laws like they'd done years before; and since we weren't the cheapskates our Agent had told them we were, they were going to leave the appliances there for us for free.

IT HELPS
NEGOTIATIONS

Making all parties feel good about each other makes a lot more sense than doing otherwise. It's positive. It can only help negotiations. It not only helps while negotiating an offer, but it will prove invaluable if a problem develops between the time an offer is accepted and the closing date. It's always easier to resolve problems if the parties feel good about each other.

When you succeed at making other people feel good about each other, they also feel good about you and vice versa. **Being able to make all parties feel good about each other consistently, is one of the distinguishing characteristics of a master negotiator.**

CHAPTER 21

AVOIDING
PRE-MATURE DEADLOCK

When you're presenting offers, always keep the focus

on the problem and stay relaxed. When you're calm and at ease, negotiations are less likely to reach an impasse prematurely, because the other side is not so apt to take a firm stand that will bog down the process.

THE "WHAT IF" APPROACH

If things appear to be reaching a deadlock, don't get uptight. Most deadlocks concern money, but there's usually a number of other variables that can be adjusted to make an agreement possible.

Many times, negotiations break down unnecessarily. They become stuck on one issue and get deadlocked because of it. With a little ingenuity many of these deadlocks can be overcome by using a negotiating technique called "Linking Alternatives". In its simplest form, it's what I refer to as the "What If" approach.

"What if my Buyer goes back through your bank for his mortgage? Won't that give you about $2,000 dollars more, since you can get the payout penalty waived if we do that?" Or, "What if my Buyer took possession in November instead of December? Would that not give you about $1,800 more since you won't have to pay the mortgage, utilities and taxes for the extra month?" Or, "What if we let you keep the fridge and stove?" and so on.

Suggest no more than one "What If" alternative at a time, making sure to emphasize its benefit to the other side. Be sure as well to emphasize the fact that it carries a cost to both you and your Buyer in terms of money or inconvenience or both. Otherwise it will be perceived as having little value and something you were willing to give up for nothing.

A CONSISTENT
NEGOTIATING BLUNDER

Let me caution you however, about the use of this approach. Using this technique at the wrong time in the negotiating process, is one of the most consistent negotiating blunders I've seen Real Estate Salespeople make over the years when presenting offers.

Before you can use this technique you have to know two things. First of all, you have to know **exactly** what objections the other side has to your offer. Secondly, you need to know you have agreement on all the other points you've put forth. Otherwise you'd simply be letting the other side know prematurely what you're willing to give up.

DOUBLE-BARRELED
QUESTIONS

The best way to accomplish this is to ask one or two well thought out double-barreled questions in a calm and friendly way. Double-barreled questions are questions which have two purposes. In other words obtaining the right answer to a double-barreled question will accomplish more that one objective for you.

In this case we want the answer to our questions to:

1) clearly identify and segregate the objections, and

2) at the same time give closure to all the other points in our offer.

AN
EXAMPLE

If for example, you're presenting an offer and the Sellers are all shook up about the price, you might ask them, "Aside from the price, is there any other reason why you wouldn't accept this offer as it's written right now?"

The answer to this question will let you know if there's only one, or if there are several objections you have to deal with. If they respond that another reason they couldn't accept the offer is that they can't let the fridge go, because it's custom made for their handicapped child to use when he's home by himself, you simply follow up with a similar question which includes the new objection.

In this case you might ask, "So are you telling me that if the price were right and the refrigerator was excluded, you'd accept the offer the way it's written right now?" When they respond that they'd accept the offer except for those two reasons, you've accomplished both your objectives. You've clearly identified and segregated their objections. At the same time you've obtained agreement on all the other terms of your offer.

You're now in a position — and only now — to use the "What If" approach effectively. This will usually ensure that negotiations continue to progress without becoming deadlocked or getting bogged down prematurely.

CHAPTER 22

CLOSING TECHNIQUES

When negotiating offers and counter-offers there are a

variety of closing techniques one can use depending on the circumstances. In this Chapter we'll deal with a few that have proved effective for me over the years.

BE POSITIVE
AND FAIR

Always concentrate on presenting your position as being positive and fair — rather than trying to prove the other side wrong.

Let's assume we have an offer on a badly overpriced listing. Usually when a listing is obviously overpriced the Listing Agent is the first to admit it. They are generally happy that if nothing else, in the process of presenting an offer, you can give them a little help in getting a price reduction if your offer doesn't go together. After all, if the Seller won't come down in price, they're not likely to earn a commission for their efforts.

When I get an offer on a listing which is obviously overpriced, I tell the Lister in advance that when I present my offer I want his cooperation, because if nothing else, my Presentation will help him get a price reduction if my offer doesn't result in a deal.

EXPLAIN
THE PURPOSE

I point out that when I present my offer I'll be going over the computer printouts that my Buyer analyzed before making his offer on the property. I explain the purpose will be to convince the Seller my Buyer has made a fair offer — not to prove the listing is over priced. I assure him that I'll present it in a manner that will make him look good.

Instead of taking a list of repairs along and knocking the Seller's home to try and prove it's priced too high, take a computer prepared Market Analysis with you to convince the Seller that your Buyer has made a fair offer.

The most important point here — and I want to really emphasize this — is to tell the Seller you want to show him why your Buyer thought he was making a fair offer; not that you think his home is overpriced or he shouldn't be asking so much.

Point out the information you're going to cover with him is readily available to anyone who wants it; that your Buyer reviewed it before making his offer, just as he'd probably do if he was purchasing a home today.

EXPLAIN
SIGNIFICANCE OF DATA

Give the Seller a copy of each printout. Of course it helps if you or your Buyer highlighted and marked them up a bit when analyzing them earlier. Explain the abbreviations, and lead them through the lists of comparables one at a time. Go over the solds, the actives and the expiries with them, just as if you were doing a Market Analysis.

Don't assume the Seller understands the meaning or significance of the data contained in the printouts. Explain that the recent solds demonstrate what a Buyer is willing to pay for similar homes today.

Point out that the actives show us what his competition is, and that included among them, are some other homes your Buyer could purchase, and considered before making the offer on his home.

Tell him the expiries demonstrate clearly what Buyers are not willing to pay for a home like his. Ask him if based on this data, which he has just analyzed himself, does he not agree your Buyer has made a fair offer.

It's almost impossible for any reasonable person to totally ignore the facts. If your Buyer has made a reasonable offer and this technique doesn't clinch an acceptance, it will certainly help get you a reasonable counter-offer.

THE
GAMBLING TECHNIQUE

Another technique that I've used quite successfully over the years, I've named the "Gambling Technique". It's particularly effective if you're dealing with a Seller who's on the conservative side and suggests signing a good offer back for a few thousand more, risking a sure sale in the process.

I explain that I'm not there to pressure the Sellers into making a decision of any kind. It's their home and only they can decide whether or not to accept the offer. I explain that I have an obligation to give them all the information I know of, that will help them make the best decision possible.

In this case it simply depends on how big they like to gamble. I point out that Mr. & Mrs. Buyer have just agreed to buy their home for $X. If they accept the offer their home is sold — right now. End of story. If they don't accept it, they're gambling that Mr. & Mrs. Buyer will pay more, and we have no assurance whatsoever that they will.

If Mr. & Mrs. Buyer won't pay more and decide to buy something else, then they're gambling that someone else will pay a little more than Mr. & Mrs. Buyer have agreed to pay.

The fact is, there's no assurance that someone else will even pay as much. So I simply ask them, "Do you think it's worth taking that big a gamble when you know your home is sold for sure, if you accept this offer as it's written right now?"

THE TIME
ELEMENT TECHNIQUE

If the home has been on the market for a while I use what I call my "Time Element" technique. This technique can be incorporated into the "Gambling Technique" or it can be used on its own depending on the Seller and the circumstances. The longer the home has been on the market the more effective this technique will be. If it accomplishes nothing else it will usually help get a more reasonable counter-offer.

I start off by asking a question such as, "Mr. Seller your home has been on the market about two months now, right?" Then I point out that it's taken two months to find someone who wants to buy their home. If we let these Buyers get away, the odds are pretty good that it might take another two months to find someone else who wants to buy it.

Then I ask them, "Taking into account what we just talked about, do you think it's worth taking a chance on losing a sure thing like you have in your hands right now?"

THE PEACE
OF MIND TECHNIQUE

Several years ago my husband and I moved to a new location and decided we should buy a home. We had moved from an area where the real estate market was somewhat depressed to an area where the market was booming.

Because of the vast difference in values my husband became your typical Buyer. He decided all homes in the new location were overpriced and weren't worth what they were selling for. We made low ball offers on one house after another, until I got so sick of looking at homes I couldn't take it any more.

Finally, after looking at I don't know how many homes over a two month period, we got a counter-offer on a home that was within $3000 of what my husband said he'd pay.

By this time both the kids and myself were really fed up with not knowing where we'd be living. The uncertainty was draining us emotionally. I decided it was worth the extra $3000 to get some "peace of mind" and convinced my husband to go ahead with the deal.

One of the results of that experience was the development of my "Peace of Mind" close, which was basically what I used to convince my husband to accept that counter-offer I just referred to.

Since then I've used this technique over and over again with much success. It's especially effective with out-of-town Buyers who are facing all kinds of deadlines, and need that final push when you're trying to close on a counter-offer.

I tell them my story and relate it to their own situation by asking them something like this, "Isn't having the "peace of mind" of knowing you don't have to come back to Calgary again to find a home; the "peace of mind" of knowing you can get the children registered in school; the "peace of mind" of being able to make your moving arrangements; and the "peace of mind" of being able to get on with your life with no more worries, worth more than the few dollars we're talking about here?"

THE BUY-BACK
TECHNIQUE

Another technique that I've found to be priceless is one I call the "Buy Back" technique that I picked up from Jerry Bresser years ago. It's invaluable when you're negotiating with a Seller who tends to be on the stubborn side about getting his price.

I tell the Seller that right at this very moment their home is sold. Mr. & Mrs. Buyer have just agreed to buy their home for $150,000 dollars. If they accept the offer their home is sold. It's over and done with!

If they don't accept the offer, in effect they're becoming real estate speculators, buying their home back for the same price Mr. & Mrs. Buyer agreed to pay them and putting it back on the market hoping to make a profit.

I point out that based on their proposed counter-offer the profit would be $3,000 dollars. Then I ask them this question. "If I came here tonight to talk to you about investing the amount of money you've been offered by the Buyers, in another property similar to this one, on nothing more than the hope that someone might pay you a profit equal to your counter-offer of $3000, would you buy that property from me on that basis?" Then I shut up and wait for a response. Sometimes it's a long wait, because this really gets them thinking and usually works wonders.

THE MULTIPLE
OFFER TECHNIQUE

Most of us who've been in this business for a while, have been involved in the sale of properties where more than one offer was being presented at the same time. In really overheated markets, it's not unusual to have multiple offers on nearly every listing. Here's a little technique that has always given me the edge when I'm one of several Salespeople presenting offers on a listing at the same time.

When I go to present an offer in this situation I always take my Buyer with me in the car. At the conclusion of my offer Presentation I tell the Listing Agent and the Seller, that if they want a fast answer I'm in a position to get it for them, because I have my Buyer with me in my car right in their driveway or parking lot.

Seldom are the other Agents in a position to obtain an immediate answer so I usually win. Since I started using this approach when competing on multiple offer Presentations, it's rare that my offers don't get acted on by the Seller before the others.

GENERATE
MULTIPLE OFFERS

Here's a great way to generate multiple offers on your listings. When you get a call from another Salesperson that they have an offer on one of your listings, call all the other Salespeople who have shown the property in the past two weeks. If it's a larger, more expensive property, go back four weeks.

Tell the Salespeople you've got an Offer and what time it's being presented. Explain you wanted to let them know so they could tell their Buyers and give them the opportunity to make an offer.

Of course, the type of market you're experiencing at the time has a bearing on how frequent this will be successful. However, from conversations I've had with other Top Agents, it seems that about one out of five times this technique will attract a second or third offer.

WHEN
NEGOTIATIONS SUCCEED

When negotiations result in a completed transaction, it's important you reassure your Client they made a good deal. Give them plenty of ammunition to justify it to themselves and others.

Resell the amenities, the neighborhood, the home itself and the features they like about it. It's important your Clients have a positive feeling about the transaction at the conclusion of the negotiations. If they don't, they won't deal with you again and won't refer others to you.

Be sure they understand the deal they made was fair to both sides.

WHEN
NEGOTIATIONS FAIL

Sometimes negotiations fail to produce the results we were hoping for, and have to be broken off. If you're simply rehashing problems and getting nowhere, it's time to break them off. But do it tactfully. Don't say "This is it. Take it or leave it." Those are offensive words and can't possible do any good.

Remember no one is happy when negotiations fail. In most cases both parties are disappointed. Leave on a friendly note and make them feel good about their property and your Buyers.

Tell them they have a beautiful home, what great people you're Buyers are, how the home suits them perfectly and how badly you feel for both of them that the deal couldn't go together.

Tell them that if your Clients' situation changes you'll get in touch immediately and you hope they'll do likewise if their situation changes. Always keep the door open for the possibility of future dealings between the parties.

THE ZAP'EM
TECHNIQUE

No matter how thorough we are, even the best of us get fooled occasionally. Over the years I have to admit the odd impossible Seller and Buyer has crept into my happy family of Clients and Customers. The important thing is to recognize these types for what they really are and take appropriate action quickly. If you don't, they'll drive you insane — and bankrupt you too!

If by chance, we find ourselves dealing with totally unreasonable Buyers and Sellers, no matter what techniques we use they will not be effective. The only sensible technique is to zap'em — or in other words, get rid of them completely.

.

CHAPTER 23

TELEPHONE NEGOTIATIONS

Negotiating with someone over the phone can be dangerous. Many things can go wrong. For one thing, it's easier to misunderstand someone over the phone. It's also a lot easier for both sides to say "no" over the phone, than in face-to-face situations.

SOMETIMES
IT MAKES SENSE

Under certain circumstances, however, it makes sense to negotiate by phone. The most obvious in our business is when one of the parties is out-of-town. Another is when there aren't many issues to negotiate and the issues are minor. If we have an acceptable price, we're one day out on the possession date and that's the only issue involved, it makes good sense to negotiate that issue by phone and simply get the signatures when it's settled.

If we have a ridiculously low offer, we know the Buyer won't come up and we won't get a deal in any case, we might as well present it by phone. Under these circumstances we'd be wasting our time if we did otherwise.

BE FULLY
PREPARED

There are a few prerequisites to keep in mind if we're going to negotiate by phone. First of all be fully prepared. Whether you're making the call or receiving an expected call, be just as prepared as if you were going to negotiate face-to-face.

If you receive an unexpected call to negotiate with someone, listen to the full story, then hang up and call back when you're fully prepared. Never let yourself get pressured into negotiating over the telephone if you're not thoroughly prepared.

Have everything that you're going to need at hand before the call or when you call back — files, documents, calculator, paper and whatever else you'll need.

BE SURE
YOU TAKE NOTES

Be sure you take notes. Make a written record of everything that's discussed. Don't trust your memory. After you've concluded the negotiations confirm the content of your notes with the other side, so there's no misunderstanding later on.

HANG UP
AND CALL BACK

Always have a good excuse ready so you can hang up and rethink your strategy if things aren't going well. I preface every telephone negotiation with a comment that I might be hanging up and calling them back before we're done, to make a phone call or two. If things go well I don't hang up until we're done. If they don't go well I excuse myself, hang up, make a phone call or two to shake the cobwebs loose, rethink my strategy and then call back.

It goes without saying that any agreement reached as a result of negotiating by telephone should be confirmed in writing as soon as possible after the negotiations have taken place. In this age of high technology this should be possible almost instantly, with originals following by courier the next day.

A
DRAMATIC LESSON

The telephone can be our best friend when it comes to negotiating appointments with prospects we call, or with those who call us. The important thing is that we use it properly. I had this lesson driven home to me rather dramatically shortly after I started in the real estate sales business.

An old pro who has long since passed away and who always had plenty of appointments, taught me one of the most valuable negotiating lessons I've ever learned. I've probably obtained more listings and sales over the years as a result of it than any other advice I've ever been given.

I had been telephone canvassing for several days without success when he called me aside and said, **"I've been watching you use the telephone young lady and you're going about it all the wrong way. If you want a person to sign a contract you have to put a pen in his hand instead of a receiver in his ear."**

"In the sales business the telephone should be used for only two purposes. First it should be used to make appointments. Every time you pick up that receiver you should remind yourself that you're picking it up to get yourself another appointment. Secondly it should be used to tell your spouse what time you'll be home for dinner. Any other use of the telephone during working hours should be seriously questioned."

On the surface that advice appears to be narrow and somewhat extreme. But if we do as my old friend suggested and question the necessity of all the other purposes we use the phone for each day, we can't help but be more productive as a result.

And I know from experience that we'd all have more appointments, if every time we picked up the receiver we followed my old friend's suggestion and said to ourselves, **"I'm picking this up to get an appointment."**

The moral of my old friend's story is this: *Sometimes we have to negotiate with ourselves!*

CHAPTER 24

ASK MORE — GET MORE

In closing I'd like to discuss one final negotiating

truism and that is, "The more you ask for — the more you'll get".

In one experiment conducted by the Harvard Graduate School of Business Administration, one group of negotiators was told that the typical negotiator in their position got $7.50 for a certain service and another group of negotiators was told that $2.50 was normal.

In addition to being told what amount the typical negotiator in their position got, both groups were told they were free to charge as much as they could get for the service. These two groups then negotiated with people who came into a room that was divided in two, to purchase the service in question.

The outcome of this exercise was rather interesting to say the least. The negotiators who aimed for $7.50 got close to that amount — and the ones who aimed for $2.50 got close to that amount. Other experiments and studies have been carried out with similar results. The fact is that Salespeople tend to negotiate for what "they" perceive to be the bottom line.

WE NEGOTIATE MINIMUMS
INSTEAD OF MAXIMUMS

Real Estate Salespeople are no different. We negotiate for the minimum rather than the maximum all the time. We do this continually with both Buyers and Sellers.

We negotiate with Sellers to get them to pay the minimum commission set by our Company. If our Company doesn't have a minimum, we try for the average which is prevalent in our area. Seldom if ever, do we negotiate for the maximum we can get!

Not only do we negotiate minimum commissions, but we're constantly negotiating the expiry dates on the listings we write, for the minimum period of time rather than the maximum.

We do the same thing when we're negotiating the use of our most precious commodity — our time! We go to the Seller's home to present offers rather than have them come to our office. We rush out to show homes to people because they demand it, rather than have them come for a Buyer Interview so we can qualify them properly first, and ensure our time is not being wasted. And it goes on and on, ad infinitum.

PURE PROFIT
LEFT ON TABLE

In the process we leave thousands and thousands of dollars in pure profit for ourselves on the table. Those who cut commissions on every deal, frequently leave the difference between a good year and bad year on the table. Every year a new group of Agents negotiate themselves right out of the real estate business, because they negotiate the minimum for themselves instead of the maximum.

As I stated elsewhere in this book, one of the main reasons for this situation is, that the industry as a whole does a poor job of teaching Salespeople to be good negotiators. As a result many Salespeople fail to succeed in our business at all, and many others earn but a fraction of what they should be earning selling real estate.

I know because I've been there myself. For years I earned far less than I should have, because I was less than proficient when it came to negotiating on my own behalf. I never, ever, negotiated for the maximum.

THE POEM
THAT SAYS IT ALL

Then one day I read a book entitled "Think and Grow Rich" by Doctor Napoleon Hill, that my Dad had given me some twenty years before. I came across a poem in that book that caused me to mend my ways. After reading and digesting what that poem taught, for the first time in my life, I began charging what I was worth.

That poem, which was originally written by Jessie Rittenhouse, explains better than anything else I have ever read or heard, why we should negotiate the maximum for ourselves rather than the minimum.

Today I live by what that poem teaches! I'd like to leave it with you now and dedicate it to all those in our business who negotiate the minimum for themselves, by charging less than they're worth or by cutting their commission on every deal. I hope it affects your life as profoundly as it's affected mine. And, it goes like this:

I bargained with life for a penny
And life would pay no more,
However, I begged at evening
When I counted my scanty store.

For life is a just employer,
He gives you what you ask,
But once you have set the wages
Why, you must bear the task.

I worked for a menial's hire
Only to learn, dismayed
That any wage I had asked of life
Life would have willingly paid.

Good Luck, Good Negotiating and Good Selling!

Products
By
Marilyn Jennings
and

Ordering
Information...
on the Following Pages

CD Albums

4 CD Albums by Marilyn Jennings
on Real Estate Sales,
The Championship Way

Album #1 • Negotiating to Win
           • Managing Time to Achieve Your Goals

Album #2 • Realtor Assistants —
           Everything You Need to Know!

Album #3 • A 17 Step Buyer Interview that guarantees
           loyalty, sales and income
           • "List More" Listing Strategies

Album #4 • Build Goodwill, You Can Sell
           • Networking Conventions for Profit

Order Now...

Each Album Only $99.95 plus taxes, shipping & handling.

Order all four of above albums: **Save $30.00**

(Note: Prices are subject to change without notice)
(Tape Albums available upon request)

Call our Toll Free number and leave your name; address; phone number; Visa, Mastercard, or AMEX number and expiry date; with:

PUBLISHING LTD.

CANADA & USA Dial 1-800-736-2335
NEW ZEALAND Dial 0-800-449-702
AUSTRALIA Dial 1-800-12-9096
E-MAIL office@mcjpub.com
WEBSITE www.mcjpub.com

or Write MCJ Publishing Ltd., Box 6167 Stn "A", Calgary, Alberta, Canada T2H 2L4

A Great
Promotional Idea!!

Yes!... <u>FOR BROKER-OWNER/MANAGERS</u>
Bull's-Eye Negotiating and *Championship Selling* make great "Recruiting Gifts" for Broker-Owner/Managers who want to impress new Salespeople and potential recruits.

Yes!... <u>FOR SALESPEOPLE</u>
Bull's-Eye Negotiating and *Championship Selling* make great "Thank-You Gifts" for other Salespeople when they sell one of your listings or do anything else that deserves special appreciation.

Yes!... 25% Discount off regular price of $34.95 on orders in multiples of 12 (i.e. 12; 24; 36 copies) plus taxes, shipping & handling.

Order Now...

(Note: Prices are subject to change without notice)

Call our Toll Free number and leave your name; address; phone number; Visa, Mastercard, or AMEX number and expiry date; with:

PUBLISHING LTD.

CANADA & USA Dial 1-800-736-2335
NEW ZEALAND Dial 0-800-449-702
AUSTRALIA Dial 1-800-12-9096
E-MAIL office@mcjpub.com
WEBSITE www.mcjpub.com

or Write MCJ Publishing Ltd., Box 6167 Stn "A", Calgary, Alberta, Canada T2H 2L4

Attention:
Broker-Owners and
Managers

Tired?... of trying to get everyone out to expensive functions to get the sales education you feel is needed?

Tired?... of being disappointed because the material presented by professional speakers doesn't relate to Real Estate Sales?

The Solution... an exclusive half-day Mini-Rally® conducted by Marilyn Jennings for your Salespeople, right in your own community!

Remember... Better Salespeople = Higher Profits for Broker-Owners / Managers

Acclaimed international speaker, best selling author and one of North America's leading Real Estate Salespeople, Marilyn Jennings is your Mini-Rally® Specialist. Marilyn conducts over 200 half-day Mini-Rallies® annually throughout North America, Australia and New Zealand.

To arrange a half-day Mini-Rally® for your Individual Office, Regional Meeting, Sales Conference or Real Estate Board Rally...

CANADA & USA Dial 1-800-736-2335
NEW ZEALAND Dial 0-800-449-702
AUSTRALIA Dial 1-800-12-9096
E-MAIL office@mcjpub.com
WEBSITE www.mcjpub.com

or for information write to:
MCJ Publishing Ltd.
Box 6167, Stn "A", Calgary, Alberta, Canada T2H 2L4